DIRECT SUPPORT

— FROM A —

MANAGER'S VIEWPOINT

A LITTLE DAY HABILITATION COMPANION

AMARA M. KAMARA

authorHOUSE®

AuthorHouse™ LLC
1663 Liberty Drive
Bloomington, IN 47403
www.authorhouse.com
Phone: 1-800-839-8640

Published by AuthorHouse   08/19/2014

ISBN: 978-1-4969-1442-2 (sc)
ISBN: 978-1-4969-1443-9 (e)

How to Use This Book

The real measure of effectiveness of this book lies in how much of a tool it is for Direct Support Professionals in enhancing their understanding into what direct support is and how to make it better. Here is a simple six-step guide:

1. Whether you are a newcomer to the field of direct support or have numerous years of experience with direct and indirect supports, or you are presently a direct support staff person looking for answers relevant to the actual direct support process, then this is the book for you and *reading* it will lend you a renewed grasp of a whole new perspective of the essentials of direct support.

2. This book answers many of the how-to questions with detail explanations and tools that are applied to practical direct support scenarios as well as through visual presentations to demonstrate the relationship of one concept or term to a given structure or process. The scenarios are actual examples but with hypothetical names. Apply the tools to scenarios similar to the scenarios that follow each tool in this book.

3. There are takeaways that present both summarized idea of the section before it and sometimes introduce a connecting concept in the section after it. The takeaways in this book are as concise as possible and can be used to show how vying concepts of a section fit together.

4. This book is completely focused on direct support and contains tools and strategies of how to make the process of direct support more effective. Although the materials are drawn from practical firsthand practice it would only produce effectiveness when the tools are *properly understood* prior to applying them.

5. *Practice* will bring you closer to perfection every time. It is helpful to recite the acronyms relevant to a scenario as soon as you come across

one. This can be a good way of testing the practicality of each tool in the book to everyday direct support encounters. For instance after a few practical applications, the SEAMAN technique will naturally come to mind when you are seated at a meeting for a nonverbal and severely intellectually and developmentally challenged individual; or you will know an artificial routine when you see one.

6. *Training* on window scenarios or peer to peer discussion. A window scenario is a case that represents numerous other cases like it. Select a real scenario and change any identifying information. Use the tools in the book appropriate to the scenario to do *problem solving* as a team, or *start a conversation* with a peer about the content that you find interesting. This is necessary because sometimes people grasp a concept or a system when they are part of its practical application.

To The Tireless and Selfless Work of All

Direct Support Professionals

"Enable the Disabled; Translate Disability into Ability; Capability, a winning Opportunity-Indeed a Reality"

-Dr Veena Kumari

TABLE OF CONTENTS

About The Author xiii
Acknowledgements xv
Preface xvii
Introduction xxi
Acronyms xxiii

Chapter 1

Understanding Direct Support 1
    A. Defining Direct support 3
    B. Direct Support Process and Individual Differences 5
        1) Advantage of differences 5
        2) Challenges of differences 6
            i. Negative impression 7
            ii. Dealing with negative impression 9
    C. The art of engagement 11
        1) Contact and engagement 11
            i. Hard contacts 11
            ii. Soft Contacts 12
        2) Engagement Techniques 14
    D. Chapter Summary 19

Chapter 2

Delivering Direct Support 21
    A. Staff Action 23
        1) NAMO: The features of a Staff Action 23
    B. Opportunity Approach 28
        1) Routine 28
        2) Opportunity and Routine 29
        3) Finding an opportunity within a routine 30

C. Elements of Opportunity Approach 32
   1) Daily Living Event (DLE) 32
      i. DLE and routines: 33
      ii. Types of routines 34
         1. Artificial Routines 34
            a. Role of preference in artificial routines... 35
            b. Improving an artificial routine 36
               1. Constellation of tasks 40
         2. Genuine Routine 41
            a. Reverse constellation 43
   2) Consistency 46
      i. Why consistency matters? 46
      ii. Frequency of the routine 48
      iii. Incorporating Routine and Goal 50
         1. Branching out 51
            a. Opportunity Leads (OL) 53
      iv. Making consistency work 54
   3) Goal Attainment 56
      i. Maintenance of current skills 57
D. Scenarios of opportunity 59
   1) Opportunity Time 59
   2) Opportunity Environment 59
   3) Special Occurrence Opportunity 60
E. Challenges to Opportunity Approach 62
F. Chapter Summary 63

Chapter 3

Assessing Discovery 65
A. Discovery: Furthering staff action 67
B. Types of Discovery 69
   1) Technical Discovery 69
   2) Direct Discovery 71
      i. Characteristics of responses 72
         1. Passive Response 72
            a. Causes of Passive Responses 73
            b. Improving Passive Responses 75
               i. Staged Participation 76
         2. Active Response 78
      ii. Recording Direct Discovery: 80

1. Positive discovery 81
2. Negative Discovery 82
iii. Determining Direct Discovery 85
3) Discovery Worksheet....................................... 87
C. Summary of Chapter... 89

Chapter 4

Capability Vs Preference... 91
A. Capacity vs Preference 93
1) Expectations 94
i. Personal expectations.............................. 96
ii. Family expectation 98
iii. Service providers' expectation 99
iv. The Now Factor (TNF) 101
2) Result and consequence.............................. 105
B. Preference 110
1) Types of preferences..................................112
a. Expressed Preference (EP)....................112
b. Opportunity Lead and technology software 114
2) Community Inclusion vs Community Participation...... 124
C. Capacity... 127
i. Meaningfulness vs Appropriateness 130
D. Summary of Chapter... 132

Appendix
The Case of Wendy Johns..135
Glossary
Direct Support Terms..145

ABOUT THE AUTHOR

Amara Kamara is a direct support manager at one of New York City's largest nonprofit organization that serves over 15,000 people with intellectual and developmental disabilities. Having served in direct support professional roles and grew through the ranks of direct support to a manager, Amara's own questions when he served as a direct support professional (DSP), coupled with his experience as a direct support manager afford him varying multitude of resolutions for the diverse everyday direct support situations facing those involved with providing care and support to people with special needs. All these provided the inspiration in making writing and producing the book possible.

Amara received his graduate degree in Human Services in 2010 (summa cum laude) from Capella University with concentration on Educational, Life Planning & Career Development. He also earned a second graduate degree in Intelligence Studies in 2013 (summa cum laude) from the American Military University with concentration in Intelligence Analysis. Amara has over a decade of experience in social services evaluations, eligibility determination for troubled youths, seniors, and displaced people in war-torn countries.

He is a full member of the National Organization of Human Services (NOHS) and the New York State Association for People in Supported Employment (APSE – New York State Chapter).

ACKNOWLEDGEMENTS

This book would certainly not have been possible without the help, love, and dedication of many wonderful people, including Justin Perkins, who I shadowed during my first week in the field as a Direct Support Professional.

I would also like to thank the following people who made this book possible:

My colleagues:

James Nuahn
Yeimi Korsberg
MacDonald Metzger

Thanks for your many suggestions and comments and for reading my draft and returning it on such short notice

Mary A. Darboh

For inspiring me to keep my dream of publishing this book alive. As a newcomer to the field prior to this book, your curiosity into knowing and questioning everything from context, process, to outcome challenged me into embarking on this book.

My friends and family:

You have helped me in more ways than I can recall and kept me working, even when I did not want to.

Warning-Disclaimer

This book is designed to provide resourceful guides on the direct support process specifically covering understanding into the process, the intricacies of deriving and delivering direct support, assessing discovery as a way of furthering staff action, and the discussion on how to effectively navigate the gray areas of capacity and preference.

It is not the purpose of this book to reprint all the information that is otherwise available to direct support professionals and direct support providers, but instead to complement, amplify and supplement other tools and texts already available in the field of direct support. You are urged to read all the available materials, learn as much as possible about direct support, and tailor the information to your individual needs.

Every effort has been made to make this Book as complete and as accurate as possible.

However, there may be mistakes, both typographical and in content. Therefore, this text should be used only as a general guide and not as the ultimate source of direct support information. Furthermore, this book contains information on direct support reflecting policy expectations in the field that are current only up to the printing date.

The purpose of this Book is to educate, guide, and enhance the existing approaches to direct support. The author and AuthorHouse Publishing shall have neither liability nor responsibility to any person or entity with respect to any loss or damage caused, or alleged to have been caused, directly or indirectly, by the information contained in this book.

If you do not wish to be bound by the above, you may return this book to the publisher for a full refund.

PREFACE

I have always been amazed by the *diligent* work of direct support professionals. I use the word diligent; however, the full nature of direct support cannot be captured by any single word; and maybe this is because the nomenclature of the work itself is a combination of two words that have simple literal meanings but complex in practice.

The love and patience endure in direct support are immeasurable. The expectations held across the field and the public at large regarding the direct support process is religious so much that the work of direct support professionals represents just about how much care that society as a whole has for people with special needs.

I started in the field of direct support with literally no understanding of what to do. I attended several trainings and had a few weeks shadowing a senior direct support staff that was reckoned to have proven knowledge regarding the work and the expectations embedded within it. I asked as many questions as I could but basically all of the responses that I got in return were emphases on how the safety of the individuals supersedes everything else. I still vividly remembered my shadower telling me to concentrate on knowing my individuals, their likes and dislikes, knowing and understanding any behaviors and the triggers to those behaviors. Still unrelentingly enquiring, I asked about how the individuals' disabilities affect the teaching methods, levels of interaction, what was I supposed to be teaching them, and how was I going to be teaching them.

For once my shadower thought that I was not ready to provide direct supports. But observing my demonstrated interest in working and wanting to know how to work better with the individuals, he told me that I would have gotten a hang of it but repeatedly cautioned me to be careful no matter how certain I was in the process of helping. After few days of shadowing, questions continue to develop in my head and I continued to ask them. At one point, the shadower turned to me and asked, *what did you say at the interview for the position before you were hired?* Do you remember the reasons for which you were hired? I said yes, and he said so then you should apply those reasons in the form of a responsibility to whomever you will be assigned to work with.

From that moment I became overwhelmed not by the everyday tasks but by the known unknowns because in addition to the job descriptions that I signed up on I was also required to do almost anything that is modified by subjectively immeasurable words like *appropriate, meaningful, empowering*, and just about any catchall term there is requiring me to treat the person receiving support as peers while at the same time teaching and exposing them to things that are reminiscent to those words.

After two weeks of shadowing and a full week of training earlier, I took control of my responsibilities in terms of applying the very reasons for which I was hired—to empower and protect individuals with intellectual and developmental disabilities that I serve. There was no scarcity of trainings and other materials on how to use the troves of available resources to empower and protect the people receiving services.

However, I soon started feeling abandoned not necessarily that I was; but there were times when I would feel as though I have been taken to the Kennedy Space Center, being shown the various models of spacecraft, asked to pick my choice of models, and simply handed the operation manual for flying the spacecraft into the space station.

Here, I was with all the trainings and resources that I needed in the ideal world. A lot of needed emphases are made on ensuring safety and the individual's overall quality of life. But for one fact, safety or maintaining the individual is well assured because as a new comer to the field then, all I could do was to be careful as I was trained and advised to do but for some staff who felt comfortably complacent in their responsibilities were the ones who erred on the side of knowing than caution. However, improving the quality of life for the individuals remains an impregnated package that is eventually a career-long process requiring deeper understanding, appreciation, and implementation.

Now the more people that I have interacted with, the more the question there is about what constitutes the quality of life and how those things that constitute quality of life can be gained or maintained on an individual basis. I have always searched for and asked questions about literature entirely devoted to direct support and how to make direct support effective which meant that I was looking beyond the materials and stimulations currently in the field to how effectively the relevant resources can be applied to a particular individual.

The kernel of this book is drawn from my practice in the field reflecting actual situations of reacting to and squiggling everything that I had encountered as it specifically relates to the direct support process. I continue to challenge myself to find answers that can be used to address individual challenges that stand in the way of an effective direct support. This book has four chapters centered entirely on the actual practical process of direct support. It provides practical advice on how staff actions can be effective, and contains richly visual presentation highlighting overlapping relationships between the different components of the direct support process. The major components of the process of direct support covered include the subject of Understanding Direct Support; Delivering Direct Support; Assessing Discovery; and Capacity vs. Preference. There is an Appendix which shows how the tools discussed in the book can be applied. The Appendix consists of an actual day habilitation case in which most of the concepts from chapters 1 through 4 are applied. Additionally, there are real life scenarios under each chapter and subchapter to help explain the concepts as comprehensively as possible. Finally, there are Takeaways scattered throughout the book that present a condensed central idea of pertinent concepts; as well as chapter summary at the end of each chapter.

INTRODUCTION

Group Day Habilitation (GDH) is one of the platforms of the wholesale social model movement emphasizing full community integration for individual with intellectual and developmental disabilities. One of the nuclei of GDH is to provide the most natural and stimulating settings in which supports that protect and empower the people receiving services are delivered.

From the need to organize a culture of engagement, to negotiating and prioritizing the pressing needs over the non-immediate ones, to rendering individualized support that enhances the individual's skills and choice-making ability, the challenges are enormous in GDH settings. Also in addition to all of those things that are nonnegotiable is ensuring that the safety and quality of life remain atop of the list of provisos.

The only possible way that GDH programs meet those challenges is by carefully crafted engagement with the people receiving services through direct support. Luckily, there is no shortage of information as well as stimulation in the field of habilitation or amongst direct support professionals (DSP). There are tools like the Person-Centered Planning (PCP) approach; Training and Education of Autistic and Related Communication Handicapped Children (TEACCH), The Council on Quality and Leadership Personal Outcome Measures (CQL-POM) approach, to name a few that have all been around a longtime and in the right direction. Almost all of the current tools in the field make available hundreds of resources relating to what kinds of information to look out for before and during the direct support process, and how those kinds of information can be used to derive appropriate care plan that reflects the individual true preference, capability, and dreams.

But imagine your stay at a five star hotel. Imagine breakfast, and feeling that you are being treated differently to breakfast despite all of the resources and the excellent services that one would expect from hotels of such ranking. Then you asked yourself, why am I being serviced differently? Could it be because that the particular person serving you is lacking the high class training offer to the hotel's workers or maybe the trainings are not culturally competent? Or it is such that the breakfast menu is so rich that the workers care little about the approach used in serving their guests? Or maybe, there is something missing that has to do with how the workers apply their training?

The available information in the field is abundant like those available to workers at the five-star hotel service you stayed at in the example above. Sometimes there are marathons of trainings on how to select from and use the relevant information available to direct support professionals (DSP). There is also a wealth of information about how to individualized support, how to derive person-centered support plans, and even how to formulate methodology for applying the relevant information to support a person receiving services to reach a target goal and skill.

However, there is a much bigger question of what approach is used in rendering the everyday supports to the individual. Like the hotel scenario above, you have put in your orders indicating exactly what you want, and a hotel worker even came up to you to personally take your orders. Shouldn't it matter how your order is serve to you? Or if the hotel services its guests in a particular way that does not meet your unique needs, shouldn't the service delivery be more personalize after paying for the five-star service? Should the personalized service only be limited to taking your orders and not to its delivery? This book provides the approach of how direct support *orders* should be taken and delivered. It also provides a deeper understanding into the actual direct support process by presenting techniques for improving the experience of the people served.

ACRONYMS

AR   *Active Response*: A characteristic of response that is displayed by action and progress related to reaching the individualized goal.

DLE   *Daily Living Event*: Refers to both an undertaking and the steps involve in completing it by an individual.

EP   *Expressed Preference*: A preference that is communicated by the individual receiving services through any mode of communications that is unique and perfectly understood by the individual and anyone part of providing support.

IP   *Implied Preference*: A preference that is inferred from an individual's action, his unique circumstances as well as from his past history of similar preference adopted if the individual cannot communicate in any ways due to severe inability to produce an expression.

NAMO   *Needs, Autonomy, Methodology, & Opportunity*: Refer to the features that must be contained in every staff action in order to make the direct support process more effective in producing needed reactions toward the attainment or maintenance of the individualized goal.

ND   *Negative Discovery*: A category of discovery whereby there is an obstruction that interferes with the application of staff action or with the individual's accomplishment of part or all of the components of the target goal.

OA   *Opportunity Approach*: A technique for understanding both routines and the opportunities that routines serve in the direct support process.

OL   *Opportunity Lead*: Any attraction in the form of clues, hints, stimulations, and trails of activities that are intended to capture an individual's attention and cultivate his interest in an activity.

PD   *Positive Discovery*: A category of discovery in which an individual cooperates to exposure, or accomplishes a part or all of the target goal.

PR   *Passive Response*: A characteristic of response that demonstrates no attempt, ability, or willingness on the part of the individual to initiate the task.

RIETE   *Repeat, Imagine, Express, Think, & Engage*: A technique for dealing with negative impression by endeavoring to gain conscious awareness of the negative thoughts and feelings that might be directed at an individual receiving services.

SEAMAN   *Safety, Empowerment, Ability, Medical/Clinical, Agreement, & Needs Manifested*: This is the golden rule of Implied Preference that states that the preferences adopted for a nonverbal individual must be the best of available alternatives such that the individual would have reasonably made similar preferences if only there was the ability to express so overtly.

TNF   *The Now Factor*: A specific skill that is formulated based on the individual existing capability by streamlining all of the many expectations to derive a preference that fits within the realm of the individual's existing capabilities.

chapter

Understanding Direct Support

OBJECTIVE OF THIS CHAPTER

By the end of this chapter, you will be able to demonstrate:

1. Knowledge and appreciation of what the work of direct support entails
2. Skills at dealing with the challenges and advantages of differences
3. Ability to navigate the difficulty of interacting with an individual and establishing effective engagement.

A

Defining Direct support

Direct support is an art of engagement concentrated toward safeguarding and empowering a person receiving support services. It is an applied care rendered to people who are challenged in meeting personal daily living events completely on their own. The core of direct support is hands-on upkeep through engagement crafted based on the needs and unique features of the person being supported. Although the core of direct support is the same across the support relationship, the process itself can mean different things to different individuals. While it serves some individuals only to provide social, behavioral, and community awareness improvements, for others it means complete dependence ranging from support for activities of daily living, to monitoring and maintaining a healthy check, to being the only source of daily life support.

1. Objectives of Direct Support:
   - ✓ Helping individuals to gain skills that empower them to become participating members of their communities.

   - ✓ Engaging individuals in an inclusive, ordinary, respectful, and safe manner.

   - ✓ Fostering support conditions that allows unique individual growth through exposure to community oriented learning opportunities.

   - ✓ Planning and delivering supports in a way that reflects conditions for growth based on individual learning opportunities.

2. Direct Support Process

The direct support process is a practice that is:

   - ✓ A continuously evolving engagement with an individual based on both the individual's level of ongoing development and the provision of relevant assistance to match those developments.

✓ Characterized by unique interactions at very distinguishing levels of functioning.

✓ Embedded with stimulation through effective engagement.

The Merriam-Webster dictionary defines *stimulation* as "to make (a person) excited or interested in something."[1] The direct support process is centrally about involving a person either into developing a new skill, maintaining an existing one, or helping to keep up with routines (medical or otherwise) that the individual would not otherwise do by themselves without prompts or encouragement. Irrespective of the person's capability, DSP get the person doing things by creating awareness or interest in matters for which the direct support was sought. Stimulation is one way to make direct support possible. It can be sought through exposure to timely experiences that would eventually lead to the development of interest in the given matter. An effective stimulation requires constructive direct engagement with the person receiving services.

Takeaway—1

Direct support is based on engagement with the individual receiving services. However, the use of any specific etiquette of engagement does not necessarily ensure effectiveness as there are no two persons with the same engagement pattern or reaction thereto.

---

[1] "Stimulate - Merriam-Webster Online." 2005. 2 Apr. 2014 <http://www.merriam-webster.com/dictionary/stimulate>

B

Direct Support Process
and Individual
Differences

The uniqueness of the individuals receiving services creates both the advantages and challenges to direct support.

1. Advantage of differences

   The advantage of individual differences adds richness that stems from the fact that any given type of delivery methodology or process can be used to support more than one person by individually customizing the process to suit each person uniquely.

Takeaway—2

The more customization that is done to a process the more new versions of it is created. A new way of doing things ushers in renewed perspectives of viewing a given situation differently.

DSP must think harder through the process and about the nature of their helping relationships for the deeper the consideration the clearer the understanding.

Consider the processes used to support two individuals who love necklace jewelry making:

Scenario 1.1   *Customizing Direct Support Process—Jenny*

Jenny is being supported in enhancing her jewelry making skills. The methodology that the DSP uses to support Jenny to make her jewelry making goal possible includes inspiring Jenny through exposures to various designs of necklaces, visiting art and jewelry centers; DSP also presents Jenny with visual of necklaces and gives her the opportunity to purchase or be part of purchasing the needed materials. DSP sets aside Jenny's own toolkits which Jenny is very proud to have her name labeled on. Jenny likes to be provided commendation and prompts/reminders on the pattern and size of the jewelry; and she responds well to facilitation when provided in a calm voice.

Scenario 1.1a   *Customizing Direct Support Process—Marley*

Marley loves and enjoys the same jewelry making activity and is working on enhancing his skills just as Jenny. However, unlike Jenny, Marley likes exploring videos and online resources about making various kinds of patterned necklaces. While the DSP presents Jenny with visuals, Marley does not accept that but he likes browsing through hundreds of online visuals and printing out his chosen ones with the DSP prompts. Marley likes to store his materials at his own spot and is very particular about orderliness; and he does not like to share his materials due to which DSP sets aside only the tools that Marley will need and let him lock them up and keeps the keys with himself while the DSP keeps the spare.

In both scenarios, the DSP customizes the process to involve each individual in participating and successfully completing the jewelry making process. The DSP achieves this by creating the opportunity, exposure, and relevant facilitation to empower both Jenny and Marley in their own unique ways.

2.   Challenges of differences

At times, challenges arise out of the uniqueness of the individuals through the difficulty embedded in balancing the whole individual and what he/she is really about, with what we hold to be true.

Often what we hold to be true is our impression of the person even before we have engaged and interacted with the person.

Diagram 1: DSP's impression of Marley *before* meeting

He's difficult; he bites, hits, and doesn't like X, Y, Z

Before meeting the individual receiving services, impression or expectations are already formed.

On the left, the DSP has already formed an impression of Marley. DSP's initial interaction is focused on confirming or disconfirming his impression of Marley. DSP does not really know what Marely is thinking or feeling.

UNKNOWN

Marley DSP

Marley, an Individual receiving services

Takeaway—3

DSP must first engage the individual in order to understanding who the individual is and what he or she is really about.

    i.   Negative impression

Sometimes based on our interaction with the individual our impression improves, but other times our impressions are so harden by what we read or what we have been told about the individual that our initial sets of engagement are conducted trying to have the individual to confirm or disconfirm what we already hold in our mind to be true. The confirmation of our impression or the lack of it lead us thinking of why the confirmation was what it was and not the opposite because in our minds, everyone cannot be wrong about what we have read or been told; and so we are set on making the individual who we really think he is or even make him whom we want to make him.

Diagram 2: DSP impression of Marley *after* meeting

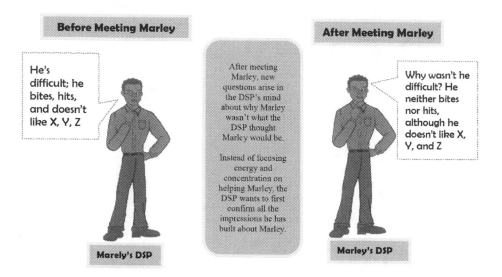

Issues with our impression occur within the interaction with the individual for the first time, as well as over an extended period of time despite the fact there have been numerous engagements that should enable the DSP to interact more constructively.

The most destructive part of all this is that the faulty impression formed about the person is transferred from one DSP to another, and overtime, a completely manufactured image is created for the individual.

The manufactured image gets stuck with the individual as opinions and facts that inform the service development meetings become unanimously adopted. Although the individual takes part in the development meetings and may be able to express his preferences, fragments of the faulty impression and opinions make their way into the habilitation plan; and direct supports are devised and provided to address the contents of the individual's plan. Being incorporated within the care plan, it gets carried over sometimes for years of support.

Takeaway—4

The impression formed before directly engaging an individual is always:

1. Overlooking; or
2. Overemphasizing something about the individual.

Either of these situations creates a suppression of opportunities that could have been used to provide the relevant support if the individual was constructively interacted with.

Impression is difficult to avoid and it is much harder to control what is heard of or read about a person as it is equally difficult to interact with a person without reflecting one's impression.

ii. Dealing with negative impression

To avoid negative impression that obstructs effective engagement, DSP must balance the whole individual, his preferences and capability with what the DSP has read or has been told about the individual by:

a. Thinking outside the box. In this case, the "box" is the impression about the individual. Think of other *positive* alternative explanations to the impression as well as the most possible natural way of interacting with the person.

b. Use ***RIETE***: DSP must endeavor to gain conscious awareness of the negative information about a person. The first step of getting rid of misconceptions or faulty representation is to first realize that the particular information is indeed problematic. Such realization comes with the conscious awareness which the *RIETE* steps will help the DSP to obtain:

i. *Repeat* the negative information about the individual to yourself. This helps in transforming your thoughts into spoken words as you listen to yourself saying them.

ii. *Imagine* what is likely said about your own unique personality. Irrespective of ability or disability, there is always something said about each of us. What is the worse of yours?

iii. *Express* positive interest in the opportunity to interact with those you wish understood you. Often we do wish to meet and interact with people who think a certain negative way about us so that they would finally come to know that we are not what they think we are.

iv. *Think* harder that the individual wants the same opportunity to interact even though chances are they may not prove otherwise in any short of period of interaction based on the level of functioning. Have it ever crossed your mind that the individual may want to disprove the negative impression about them but are significantly challenged to do so and even when they are provided the appropriate support, it takes time and consistent practice to actualize?

v. *Engage (by brokerage, making connection, identify and profile the opportunities or initiating and maintaining stimulation).* By the time you have thought harder about providing the same opportunity to interact with the individual, you should be ready to engage them by first establishing contact, engaging, and working on the staff actions with the individual. *(See The art of engagement below for details on how to engage.)*

C

The art of engagement

Engagement is an art of expressive process that is based on our contact with each other.

> ➤ The first part of every engagement is to make contact with the other person.

Contacts can be rarely challenging to initiate although initiating and succeeding with a contact are two different outcomes.

Sometimes, there are a series of successive contacts that establish the prospect for engagement and other times a single contact suffices.

1. Contact and engagement

Contact is the groundwork for engagement. It signals what engagement technique to utilize because it is always an effective way of knowing how the individual feels at any given point of the engagement. Contacts can be both *hard* and *soft* (emotional/mental).

   i. Hard contacts are those involving a physical act such as a touch that results in getting the individual's attention. Hard contact also includes those contacts that produce concrete response from the individual such as sound and sight.

Consider the following scenarios demonstrating Hard Contacts

Scenario 1.2	*Hard Contacts*

Jenny likes the iPad but she would not voluntarily ask to use the iPad nor will she accept it when the DSP is formally set to engage her with the iPad. Knowing this, the DSP usually puts the iPad, a pen and paper, and a headset right before Jenny and move away to a distance where he would be able to monitor Jenny. After a minute or two Jenny looks around and picks up the headset, plugs it into the iPad and starts to use it. DSP walks by later, sits with Jenny, picks up the pen and paper, and begins conversation about any preferred plan of action for the day and reviewing existing commitment or routines.

DSP made contact with Jenny without touch but by sight. Contact by sight conjures attentions which can be used to initiate interaction. Other examples of Hard Contacts involving seeing and hearing include a DSP placing a magazine across the table for the individual to see; the sound of the musical instrument; or signing to an individual.

    ii.   Soft Contacts are those contacts that involve emotional or mental stimulation that results in getting the individual's attention. Soft Contacts are mostly based on direct or indirect communication about things of interest to the individual.

Consider the following scenario of Soft Contact:

Scenario 1.3	*Soft Contact*

DSP sometimes fines it more challenging than usual to engage Marley in community outings from coffee shop, restaurant, to bowling or a visit to a volunteer location. Even when DSP approaches Marley and suggests a destination after Marley had refused to make any community outing choices, Marley would not accept and will usually become withdrawn if continuous efforts are made to make him understand the nature, purpose, and excitement that awaits in the outing.

> To get Marley to listen and express interest in the trip, DSP will start to talk about various destinations describing the route, purpose, the activities and sceneries to some of Marley's peers. Some of whom may or may not be interested but it is the process that is, for some reasons, actually appealing to Marley. He would listen and even pick from the DSP's list of destinations or suggest some of the places he frequents. At this point, DSP and Marley have a common goal of talking about Marley's choice and planning accordingly.

However, based on long standing relationship between most DSPs and the individuals that they support, Soft Contacts of ordinary conversation can be sufficient to set the tone for the engagement to follow.

Takeaway—5

> DSP must continue striving to gain the individual's attention in the same way the DSP's attention is sought by the individual especially as it relates to furthering the individualized goal. The more efficient the DSP is at making contact with the individual, the better understanding there will be for the technique of engagement to be effectively utilized.

After contact, what next? Contact gets the individual's attention as shown in Scenarios 1.2 & 1.3.

From the contact, DSP will have an understanding of the individual basic moods based on which the appropriate engagement techniques can be utilized.

Engagement has to be spontaneous—from the process of contact to identifying the engagement objective, and to selecting engagement technique itself. It is important that DSP is familiar with the four techniques of engagement. The objective of engagement is almost always centered on the goals that the individual is working on.

2. Engagement Techniques

From the Opportunity Approach perspective, there are four (4) engagement techniques:

- ✓ Brokerage
- ✓ Make Connection
- ✓ Identify and profile opportunities
- ✓ Maintain stimulation

Before initiating engagement, DSP must have already been aware of the purpose and objective of the engagement. Generally, the objective of direct support engagement is to support the individual stated goal or skill; *or* the focus on establishing the possibility of engagement.

While it is required to read the individual care plan before interaction, DSP must only use it as a reference of the goals but not to manufacture any image of the individual. *Complications result when DSP makes discovery other than the manufactured image formed even before an engagement was brokered.*

Table 1: Direct Engagement Techniques

Guiding Principles	Definition and application of principle

✓ *Brokerage*	• An attempt at initiating personal engagement involving *stimulating; negotiating; facilitating; and taking practical actions* relevant to the objective of the engagement.
	  • *Stimulation*: actions that would conjure the individual's interest; must be sustainable. Stimulation can neither be coercive nor aversive.
	  • *Negotiation*: exposure to resources and experiences related to the goal, and discussing plan of preferred daily actions
	  • *Facilitation*: offering clues, encouragement, and direction that make goal attainment possible.
	  • *Action*: undertake actions in furtherance of the support relationship that strengthens the engagement.

✓ *Make the connection*	• Express unconditional interest in the individual's person
	  • *Demonstrate genuine care* by showing compassion
	  • *Active attention*: listening and responding
	  • *Offering targeted help*: timely assistance
	  • *Connect with existing connection*
	  • *Persist on caring*

✓ *Identify and profile the opportunities*	*Prioritizing the routines*: before a DSP can prioritize a routine, he/she must already be aware of the individual's routine.
✓ *Initiating and maintaining stimulation*	Engagement is a continuous process and so should stimulation because stimulation creates the excitement and interests in the engagement.

The engagement technique of *Brokerage* might work with one individual at a particular time, *making connection* could work for another; or *profiling the opportunity* and so forth.

Direct engagement process is ongoing, and any of the above techniques can be used on a first engagement as well as on an ongoing basis based on the individual on any given day.

A DSP might have successfully engaged with Marley yesterday by *"maintaining stimulation"* on the things related to Marley's preference. But today, for some personal reasons, Marley appears bored with the stimulation and is not responding to any attempt to engage. The DSP can attempt to *"Make connection"* with Marley; or try to *"Broker"* an engagement with him.

The parts of direct engagement can be used jointly as well as independently of each other. Consider the following scenarios of direct engagement:

Scenario 1.4	*Engagement Technique—Connecting with existing connection*
Marley has an expressed preference for socializing with others including his DSP. When Marley gets to the day program, he proceeds to the bathroom and then picks up the box containing his routine task. Marley will sit at his table (which he calls his desks) and would not bother talking to or interacting with anyone including the DSP. Marley will only begin open up to anyone who greets him and ask about his home, and ask about church service regardless of the day of the week along the following lines: Hi Marley, how are you? How's the residence? Did you go church last Sunday? How was service? These are the "magic" phrases for Marley. From here, Marley will take over the conversation and even sing a song or two from church.	

The DSP makes the appropriate connection with Marley by both connecting with Marley's existing connection such as his residence, and the church through the technique of "Make Connection" as outlined in Table 1.

Scenario 1.5	*Engagement Technique—Brokerage*

Jenny loves current events in weather, holidays and sports games. Her favorite team is the Yankees. Her DSP recently advocated for the residence to take Jenny to a Yankee game, one of which she did attend. Jenny also loves jewelry and would independently initiate the jewelry routine with little help from DSP. Once she begins making the necklace, she does not like any kind of interaction that would distract her. Often to get Jenny's attention you will have to broker a "deal" that catch her attention by talking or asking about any news she watched on TV the night before, or about sports, or about the weather. Jenny usually provides commentary on a number of topics.

This is the Brokerage technique of direct engagement. After providing stimulation to start the engagement, negotiations, facilitation, and action can follow. See Table 1 for explanation of these steps.

Scenario 1.6	*Engagement Technique—Identify and profile the opportunity*

Mamie has a proven challenge with following direction and she also does not respond well to facilitation except where she initiates by herself. The DSP has a listing of routines that Mamie does. Although Mamie's routines are known, she is often unpredictable as to which one of her routines she would do from the moment she enters the program. She might sit at the entrance of the program and refuse to move in regardless of any kind of conversation with her; or she would just go directly into the bathroom, blinks the lights severally and then sits in one of the stalls waiting to instruct any peers who uses the bathroom and didn't flush "properly", or talk peers into not using too much toilet papers or paper tower; or begin the morning with bullying others ranging from name—calling to poking others, Turning on and off the computers or iPads even when peers are using them.

For the above scenario, DSP utilizes the *"Identify and Profile the Opportunity"* that exists in Mamie's routine because Mamie does not respond well to the techniques of "Brokerage" and "Make Connection" most of the time. DSP created the opportunity for Mamie to participate in peer supports where Mamie does brief discussion with peers providing reminders to wash hands with soap after using the bathroom, drying the hand and so forth. Mamie forfeits this participation if she insists on staying in the bathroom. Mamie is human and like everyone else, there is a soft spot. Mamie has a weakness for politeness and often gives in when she is patiently and calmly talked into foregoing or minimizing some of those routines that disrupt the affairs of others. For Mamie, firmness does not work.

Takeaway—6

No two direct engagements with any two persons will be completely the same. All levels of engagement involve unique interactions at very distinctive individual levels of functioning.

D

Chapter Summary

1. Direct support is based on engagement with the individual receiving services. However, the use of any specific etiquette of engagement does not necessarily ensure effectiveness as there are no two persons with the same engagement pattern or reaction thereto.

2. The more customization that is done to a process the more new versions of it is created. A new way of doing things ushers in renewed perspectives of viewing a given situation differently. *DSP must think harder through the process and about the nature of their helping relationships for the deeper the consideration the clearer the understanding.*

3. DSP must first engage the individual in order to understanding who the individual is and what he or she is really about.

4. The impression formed before directly engaging an individual is always (1) overlooking, or (2) overemphasizing something about the individual. Either of the situation creates a suppression of opportunities that could have been used to provide the relevant support if the individual were directly interacted with.

5. Use **RIETE**: DSP must endeavor to gain conscious awareness of all of the negative information they have about a person. The first step of getting rid of misconceptions or faulty representation is to first realize that there are indeed problematic issues. Such realization comes with the conscious awareness which the RIETE steps will help the DSP to obtain:

    i. _Repeat_ the negative information about the individual to yourself. This helps in transforming your thoughts into spoken words as you listen to yourself saying them.

ii. *Imagine* what is likely said about your own unique personality. Irrespective of ability or disability, there something said about each of us. What is the worse of yours?

iii. *Express* positive interest in the opportunity to interact with those you wish understood you. Often we do wish to meet and interact with people who think a certain negative way about us so that they would finally come to know that you are not what they think of you because you acted a certain way under certain conditions.

iv. *Think* harder that the individual wants the same opportunity to interact even though chances are they may not prove otherwise in any short of period of interaction depending on the level of functioning. Have it ever cross your mind that the individual may want to disprove the negative impression about them but are significantly challenged to do so and even when they are provided the appropriate support, it takes time and consistent practice to understand them.

v. *Engage (by brokerage, making connection, identify and profile the opportunities or initiating and maintaining stimulation).* By the time you have think harder to provide the same opportunity to interact with the individual, you should be ready to engage them by first establishing contact, engaging, and working on the staff actions with the individual. *(See the art of engagement for details on how to engage.)*

6. DSP must continue striving to gain the individual's attention in the same way the DSP's attention is sought by the individual especially as it relates to furthering the individualized goal. The more efficient the DSP is at making contact with the individual, the better understanding there will be for the technique of engagement to be effectively utilized.

7. No two direct engagements with any two persons will be completely the same. All levels of engagement involve unique interactions at very distinctive individual levels of functioning.

2

chapter

Delivering Direct Support

What happens after engagement is established

OBJECTIVE OF THIS CHAPTER

By the end of this chapter, you will be able to demonstrate:

1. The ability to formulate and apply an effective staff action
2. Understanding of the application of the Opportunity Approach to routines
3. Knowledge of finding teachable opportunities from every routines
4. Appreciation of the importance of consistency in the direct support process
5. Skills to navigate challenging behavior and other obstacles to effective engagement
6. Understanding of the relationship between routines and goals

A

Staff Action

When engagement is established with the individual, the DSP provides prearranged services directed at protecting or empowering or both by taking timely actions that enhances the skill necessary to achieving the target goals.

This is usually achieved through the actions of the DSP also known as the staff action. DSP action or staff action is usually the steps the staff takes as part of supporting and improving the individual's wellbeing.

A staff action must have four (4) features in order to ensure the person receiving services is adequately supported. These features are *Needs of the individual, Autonomy, the Methodology, and the Opportunity*; known as by the acronym NAMO.

1) NAMO: The features of a Staff Action

Every single staff action must consist of *the features of Needs, Autonomy, Methodology, & Opportunity* as defined below:

1. *Need*: The staff action must be tailored to the unique needs of the individual across relevant settings.

2. *Autonomy*: The staff action must foster independence in terms of either personal livelihood or community integration or both.

3. *Methodology*: Staff action must be definite and realistic steps relevant to attaining a very specific skill.

4. *Opportunity*: Staff action must contain the creation of the most appropriate environment, timely, sequence, and approach of how the support is provided and applied.

Diagram 3: NAMO

Staff Action

Consider the following scenario to understand the importance of the NAMO features:

Scenario 2.1	*Inadequate Staff Action (based only on preference, skills, & methodology. It is missing any opportunity)*
	Marley enjoys the company of others but only when they try well enough to have him to converse. Marley has expressed the need to be able to initiate conversation with others. As part of a person-centered process, Marley has a goal of initiating conversation. The goal is broken down into relevant skills. For the start, he is working to attain the skill of learning to *greet* as well as respond appropriately when *greeted*. The direct support methodology outlines that the DSP will regularly have conversation with Marley about greeting peers and role-play responding calmly when spoken to; and that the DSP will encourage Marley to maintain eye contact when greeting someone or responding. A number of methodological steps follow depending on the unique circumstances of Marley.

You will notice that one of the elements of NAMO is missing from the staff action in Scenario 2.1.

Consider the table below:

Table 2—NAMO: Lack of Opportunity

Need	Autonomy	Methodology	Opportunity
Greeting peers	Independent at greeting peers	Have conversation & role-play	?

The *"Opportunity"* is missing from the staff action in Scenario 2.1. This means that the staff action is lacking the creation of any appropriate environment or possibilities necessary to attaining Marley's skills, and it is also lacking timely sequence and approach of how the *"Methodology"* will be applied.

Scenario 2.1 uses the "Need-Autonomy-Methodology" format of staff action which is widely used, however, with the lack of Opportunity there is a question of how the methodologies are applied in the practical process direct support.

Takeaway—7

If a given staff action is missing any one of the NAMO features that staff action is highly unlikely to achieve the individual target skills. The reality of the steps must always be a unique reflection of actions that individual can undertake independently or has the capability to act on when the appropriate support is provided.

Consider the next scenario with identical facts as Scenario 2.1 except that an approach of delivery is added:

Scenario 2.2	*Adequate Staff Action (based on preference, skills, methodology, & opportunity. All of NAMO is present)*
	Marley enjoys the company of others but only when they try well enough to have him to converse. Marley is verbal and has expressed the need to be able to initiate conversation with others. As part of a person-centered process, Marley has a goal of initiating conversation. The goal is broken down into relevant skills. For the start, he is working to attain the skill of learning to *greet* as well as respond appropriately when *greeted*. The direct support methodology outlines that the DSP will regularly have conversation with Marley about greeting peers, and role-play responding calmly when spoken to *by engaging Marley to greet a certain identified person, observe how Marley responds and have the appropriate conversation about Marley's reaction/responds*. The methodology also states that the DSP will encourage Marley to maintain eye contact when greeting someone or responding *by role-playing greetings and eye-contact, and providing the appropriate support based on Marley's reaction*.

You will notice that the staff action in *Scenario 2.2* has all of the elements of NAMO as seen in the table below:

Table 3: NAMO – All features represented

Need	Autonomy	Methodology	Opportunity
Greeting peers	Independence at greeting peers	Have conversation & role-play	Creating the circumstance, stimulating, and facilitation by having appropriate conversation about the observation

In Scenario 2.2, the DSP applied the methodology by creating the Opportunity (i.e. *circumstances, stimulation, and facilitation*) of the target skills. Context alone is a hard procedure for most people with intellectual and developmental disability, hence, working on a skill only by the explanation of it is harder to grasp and follow.

Creating and learning in similar circumstance in which the skills can be applied is more concrete.

Takeaway—8

The Circumstance in the above scenario includes the DSP's effort to create a situation such as identifying a person to whom Marley will be speaking with in the above Scenario 2.2. *Stimulation* triggers interest in circumstance created while *Facilitation* is the efforts that is enabling and necessary for utilizing the circumstance more effectively.

B

Opportunity Approach

The opportunity approach (OA) is a technique for understanding routines and the opportunities that routines serve in the direct support process. OA is based on the teachable opportunities that are intrinsically embedded within any direct support process. The primary focus of OA is to understand the fundamental moments of the individual's interaction and how each unique moment can be utilized to improve staff support in effectively creating, maintaining, or enhancing the individual's skills.

✓ A *Direct support opportunity* is a series of daily living interactions, that when consistently explored, leads either to the attainment of emerging skills or maintenance of current ones.

The application of the Opportunity Approach encourages immersion into every possible instance in the individual's interaction with her surroundings, and using understanding from that process to tailor direct support efforts to be more appropriate and empowering. This is done by understanding the individual's interaction with everything else in an event or series of interconnected events known as a routine.

1. Routine

A routine is an individual's specific ongoing interactions that is usually built up from the individual's preference, or some behavioral or habitual happening occurring as part of a natural state of the individual.

✓ A person could have more than one routine based on time, place, or under special conditions

✓ A routine includes any activity or series of interconnected activities that requires at least minimum sets of skills or willingness on the part of the individual to complete the cycle.

The *routine* of every individual remains the single most determinant factor across the various aspects of direct support because it reflects the individual's awareness of herself and her surroundings. The individual's degree of awareness of self and surrounding provides an essential understanding of the individual's level of functioning relating to autonomy and community integration.

Consider the following scenario to provide further understanding into routine:

Scenario 2.3	*Routine*

Every morning at program, *Jenny* usually tells the day, dates, and upcoming holiday, if any. She routinely tells the weather of the next day at about end of the day before embarking on the transportation bus. *Jenny* has a habit/behavior of screaming when her environment becomes noisily saturated or overly stimulated, however, she stops screaming when she sees her DSP.

Scenario 2.3 suggests some very important information regarding Jenny's capability such as verbalization, behavioral concerns, as well as her awareness of self and her surrounding to a considerable extent. Understanding these about Jenny including things she likes to do present an opportunity for direct support.

Routines, therefore, presents an *opportunity* at enhancing interaction, relationship building, supporting the individual physical and psychological well-being, as well as planning and providing care based on emerging and ongoing needs.

2. Opportunity and Routine
   a) An opportunity is an effectively managed routine that produces a desired outcome.

   A routine cannot be effectively managed from each possible instance if the instances themselves are not anticipated, and will therefore not count as a routine.

   b) The routine is comparable to the *present state in which things are done,* so in order to plan for future enhancement of doing those things, *the routine,* which is the present, must be understood.

c) Routines can be influenced under different scenes, time of day, or relevant to specific events or persons.

In Scenario 2.3, Jenny does certain things at different times, under different situations, or in the presence or absence of a certain person. Essentially, there are certain teachable moments in each of Jenny's routine to which the Opportunity Approach can be applied to empower Jenny.

3. Finding an opportunity within a routine

Every routine presents some unique types of opportunity that can be worked with either to curtail the routine or to improve on the skills that the individual puts into the conduct of the routine.

To determine an opportunity within a routine, the following steps must be followed:

1. Identify the routine
2. Breakdown the routine to identify the steps or tasks involved in carrying it out
3. Identify the skills or qualify the willingness that makes the conduct possible
4. Select the particular skill or skills set relevant to the target goal

Consider the following scenario to help understand how to find an opportunity from an individual routine:

Scenario 2.4	*Finding an opportunity within a routine*

Rob loves dancing very much and prefers to interact with female staff to male staff. Rob dancing routine is very important to him and will initiate it by himself regardless of DSP's suggestion of alternative recreation or exercise. Rob specifically likes to imitate actresses Beyoncé and Rihanna. Dancing makes Rob happy and when he is done dancing; he can be progressively engaged in preplanned or ongoing activities. There are other unique characteristics of Rob but none stands in the way of his dancing routine. Usually, Rob does not dance to just any music; he sings songs from his favorite actresses and dances as he sings. Rob has communication and community preservation goals at the day program.

In the diagram below, you will notice how Rob's routines has been broken down to determine an opportunity:

Diagram 4: Routine Breakdown / Finding opportunity

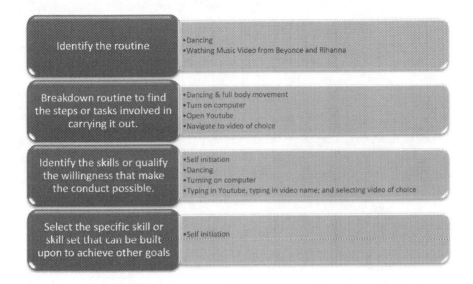

Rob's skill or willingness to self-initiate is a potential opportunity that can be used to diversify his preference by exposing him to experiences related to his current routine. Some of those things can include computer, typing, exercising, and some forms of supported employment. Rob's ability to initiate his activity or routine without any prompt or physical trigger is also essential to his habilitation goals of communication and community preservation. This means that Rob's skill at self-initiation presents an opening only if DSP consistently follow through with it to achieve the self-initiation that is required for both communication and community preservation.

Diagram 4 can also be used to find the relationship between a goal and a routine. The goal can be broken down in the same way as the routine in Diagram 4. The breakdown would provide a visual of the relationship between the goal and the preference.

If there no relation between the routine and the current goal, the goal is considered to have a virtual disconnect with the existing capability of the individual.

C

Elements of Opportunity Approach

The Opportunity Approach has three (3) elements:

- ✓ Daily Living Event (DLE)
- ✓ Consistency
- ✓ Goal Attainment or Maintenance

Diagram # 5: Opportunity Approach

   1.   Daily Living Event (DLE)

Daily Living Event (DLE) refers to both the undertaking and the steps involve in completing it by an individual. In Scenario 2.3, everything that Jenny does is a DLE.

DLE can be *specific steps* involve in the executing the task or *a series of steps* necessary to complete a part of the process of the undertaking.

Consider the following scenario to help understand DLE:

Scenario 2.5	*DLE & Steps involve in completing them*
The DLE involves in grooming one's face may include *specific steps* (like wetting a clean washcloth and rubbing the face) to completely groom the face; or it could be broken down into a *series of steps* necessary to complete a part of the process of grooming (such as (1) getting a clean washcloth, (2) opening the facet to the right temperature (3) wetting the clean washcloth (4) the rubbing the face with it.)	

Diagram #6: Daily Living Events

Specific Steps to Facial Grooming

Series of necessary steps to Facial Grooming

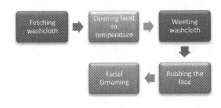

The number of steps involved in reaching the completion of a particular task vary from individual to individual based on their unique support needs.

Takeaway—12

> DSP must break down an individual's DLE into the specific steps require to complete the entire process or into steps necessary to complete part of the process based on the individual's capability and level of functioning.

---

    i.   DLE and routines:

A DLE always involves a routine. There are two parts of every routine: an *Action* which is the target activity, and a *Function* which is the manner in which that activity is carried out as well as the purpose or meaning derived from carrying out the routine:

Table # 3: Parts of a routine

Action	Function	
	Manner/Conduct	Purpose/Meaning
Grooming *(specific steps)*	Obtaining clean washcloth and rubbing face	Cleaning face/feeling better

Grooming (specific steps)	Obtaining clean washcloth	Independence
	opening facet to right temperature	Self-aware/awareness of setting
	Rubbing the face	Cleaning face/feeling better

As shown in the table above, the act of grooming can be carried out differently, and the purpose or meaning derived can be unique to different individuals. Importantly, when the steps are broken down each step must have a purpose as shown in the table above.

When the conduct of the task is broken into smaller steps as shown in Table 3, the purpose or meaning derived from each steps helps with the understanding regarding the individual's level of progress and development.

ii.   Types of routines

All routines have specific features and sequence, span, and manner in which it is carried over. The characteristics of a routine are one of the essential features that indicate whether a particular act or a series of acts is a certain kind of routine. Knowing the special features that make up the different types of routines helps with understanding the predictability of the routine.

There are two types of routine: *artificial* and *genuine*

1.   *Artificial Routines (AR)* are routines formed from preferences or learnt behavior. It includes all of those undertakings by the individual as a result of the individual's past exposures and current inclination reflecting the individual's development and emerging realities.

Consider Scenario 2.3 where Jenny usually tells the day, dates, and upcoming holiday, and routinely tells the weather of the next day at about the end of the day before boarding the transportation bus. Here, all of the undertakings are a result of Jenny's past and current exposures to things that make these undertakings possible. A behavior or habit can also be an artificial routine if it is the result of past exposures, or undertakings depicting behaviors that are reflections of past experiences that solidified the habit into the individuals.

Consider the following scenario to help understand how a behavior learnt from past exposure is an artificial routine.

Scenario 2.6	*Artificial Routine—behavior learnt from experience*
Abu has a behavior which he is said to have learnt during his time at a state institution before deinstitutionalization. At the institution, Abu and his colleagues were treated at subhuman conditions and were interacted with on that basis. They were yelled at and had no say in anything regarding themselves. As a result of those experiences, Abu is not used to being asked about what he wants to do neither formally nor informally. Also, when Abu hears loud laughter or voices even if not around his particular location he stops everything and quietly bows his head as if in submission until he receives immediate assurance from DSP that all is well. As a result, Abu spent most of his day reacting to voices that are not directed at him in any ways.	

In Scenario 2.6, the behavior of Abu is an artificial routine that has become a part of his habit as a result of his past experience while he was at the state institution. Apart from this kind of experience, behaviors are not generally considered artificial routine but rather genuine routine as explained later in the following passage.

a. Role of preference in artificial routines

Preference is the building block of an Artificial Routine.

A preference is the individual's liking or predisposition. It is an artifact of the individual's past, present, and developing life events. Often individuals with developmental and intellectual disabilities express their preferences in demonstration of experiences or responses to exposures, and their most recent past inclinations. Sometimes, an individual's experience with a given situation is so isolated that not everyone in the support circle is aware that the individual is experiencing such. It could be that the individual is being exposed to the experience by someone in his support circle. Usually, the individual will pick up on something not that he/she sees a group of people doing so but because someone in the support circle makes it appear that it is fine to do a certain thing. And gradually overtime, the individual sees it as a normalcy.

Consider the following scenario to understand the role of preference in artificial routines:

Scenario 2.7	*Role of preference in artificial routines*

Until as recently as three weeks ago, Patrice use to sign to communicate that he wants to go to the restroom. Once in the bathroom, Patrice will unfasten his belt and use the toilet accordingly whether it is number 1 or 2. A new DSP was hired a couple of weeks ago and started working with Patrice. When the new DSP accompanied Patrice in the restroom, the DSP would physically help Patrice to unfasten the belt and when Patrice get out of the bathroom stall, the DSP will help Patrice to fasten the belt again. This continued for about a few weeks. Then there was a staff reshuffle and another DSP started working with Patrice and observed that when Patrice wants to go to the restroom he would just point to the direction to the bathroom without using the sign he had been shown earlier and once in the bathroom he would stand in the bathroom stall waiting for staff to unfasten his belt if not he would wet himself instead of removing his pants and sitting on the toilet as he was doing for himself couple of weeks earlier.

From the scenario above, Patrice has been accustomed to someone fastening and unfastening his pants before and after using the restroom. However, this was so isolated that no other DSP was aware except the new DSP. Hence, Patrice's exposure to be served that way became his preference of support in the bathroom routine and when he was not afforded that support, he would wet his pants.

Artificial routines are always based on everything to which the person has ever been exposed. Sometimes the person's past was not their choice (or preference) but they however experienced it and as a result of their experience of the particular exposure has become a learnt part of what they do regularly (routinely).

b.   Improving an artificial routine

Improving an artificial routine requires understanding the things including the preference that makes the execution of the routine possible. A preference is very unique to the individual who expresses it. The individual's unique disposition is an irreplaceable tool upon which nearly all direct support efforts are formulated.

When direct support is formulated to support the individual to realize a preference, the support is actually creating, maintaining or enhancing upon the individual's current skill set as a way of meeting the preferred goal. In the case of improving the artificial routine to moving away from unproductive artificial routine, the support will be creating new alternatives based upon the individual's current capabilities.

An individual can transition from one routine to the other in demonstration of numerous preferences. DSP can adopt the following two (2) steps in the effort to transition an individual from one artificial routine to another based on existing preference:

1. Explore current set of preferences
    a. List the current preferences; and identify any experiences that can be expanded upon (To help in doing this, use Diagram #4: Routine Breakdown)

2. Exposure to new experience:
    a. If the individual's current set of preference does not contain any experience that can be expanded upon or exported into another routine, then the individual must be introduced to new things, however, exposure must be within a reasonable scope of all the things that the individual can do.

Refer to Scenario 2.8 and Diagram #7 to further explain this process.

Takeaway—13

Transitioning from one preference to another or upgrading one preference over the other as a result of unfolding development must be done based on the individual's existing capability.

Consider the following scenario to help understand transitioning between an artificial routine and a preference that is not yet a routine:

Scenario 2.8	*Transitioning between an artificial routine and a preference*

Jenny has a day habilitation routine of learning to be able to initiate conversation improving personal hygiene, and housekeeping. At an annual development meeting, Jenny expressed a preference in wanting to be a receptionist. However, to work or volunteer as a reception, Jenny must have the ability (*not necessarily the skill*) to learn how to answer phone and at minimum be able to greet or respond to visitors coming into her work area.

In the above scenario, there is a virtual disconnect between some of Jenny's current routines and her new preference. A virtual disconnect does not necessarily mean that the new preference is unattainable, it however, places an added challenge upon the attainment of a goal that is very distant from the individual's current preference and capability.

The following Venn diagram lists Jenny's current sets of artificial routines (adopted from her preference) and the new preference she recently expressed during a development meeting.

However, as you will notice from the diagram, the skills that Jenny has been working on for her socialization goal can all be applied to her new preference for working as a receptionist:

Diagram #7: Venn diagram of Preferences

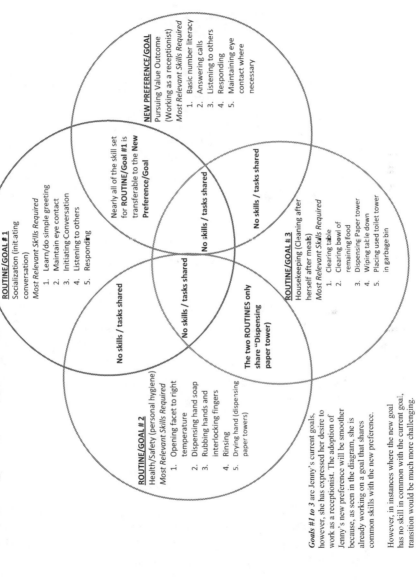

ROUTINE/GOAL #1
Socialization (initiating conversation)
Most Relevant Skills Required
1. Learn/do simple greeting
2. Maintain eye contact
3. Initiating Conversation
4. Listening to others
5. Responding

NEW PREFERENCE/GOAL
Pursuing Value Outcome
(Working as a receptionist)
Most Relevant Skills Required
1. Basic number literacy
2. Answering calls
3. Listening to others
4. Responding
5. Maintaining eye contact where necessary

Nearly all of the skill set for **ROUTINE/Goal #1** is transferable to the **New Preference/Goal**

No skills / tasks shared

No skills / tasks shared

No skills / tasks shared

No skills / tasks shared

No skills / tasks shared

The two ROUTINES only share "Dispensing paper tower)

ROUTINE/GOAL #2
Health/Safety (personal hygiene)
Most Relevant Skills Required
1. Opening facet to right temperature
2. Dispensing hand soap
3. Rubbing hands and interlocking fingers
4. Rinsing
5. Drying hand (dispensing paper towers)

ROUTINE/GOAL #3
Housekeeping (Cleaning after herself after meals)
Most Relevant Skills Required
1. Clearing table
2. Clearing bowl of remaining food
3. Dispensing Paper tower
4. Wiping table down
5. Placing used toilet tower in garbage bin

Goals #1 to 3 are Jenny's current goals, however, she has expressed her desire to work as a receptionist. The adoption of Jenny's new preference will be smoother because, as seen in the diagram, she is already working on a goal that shares common skills with the new preference.

However, in instances where the new goal has no skill in common with the current goal, transition would be much more challenging.

As shown in the Diagram 7, goals # 1 and 2 share absolutely no skills or tasks in common with the new goal. The distance between goals # 1 and 2 is a virtual disconnect that makes transitioning from the current goal to the new one practically challenging although not impossible.

Usually the current goal is always adopted based on the individual's current capability therefore new goals must not be too distant from the current goals which depicts the current level of support.

Diagram 8: New goal must have basis from current goal

However, Jenny's new preference can be incorporated by building up her current set of preferences so as to ensure continuity and dexterity.

1. Constellation of tasks

To maintain and build upon a preference, a *constellation of task* must be developed.

✓ A constellation of tasks is an interconnection between actions that are related to a person's specific preference.

Diagram 9: Constellation of the Preference of *Greeting Peer*

A constellation provides the relevant tasks or skills required to achieve a goal. The skills are arranged in clockwise sequence depicting how one skill must be successfully accomplished in order to move to the next skill in the sequence. The constellation also provides an opportunity for each task

A Constellation must be related to Action not Function

or skill in the cluster to be expanded to derive a new skill set on a need-by-need basis.

b. Derived Events

Events that serve community integration as an outcome are derived events. In addition to the individual's everyday experiences with peers and DSP, a Derived Event is a form of exposure that is only concentrated toward community integration which involves both community inclusion and community participation. The outcome is derived from the individual's involvement in the event itself. It is however called derived events so as to distinguish it from other events that are mere community inclusion.

✓ Derived events are interactions with the community that creates experiences based on the individual's participation and interests in such community engagements.

The core of derived events is to cultivate belongingness with the community.

A perfect example is the artificial routine derived from an individual's experience with volunteering and participation in community shows and programs.

Person Centered Outcomes are also derived events because they are usually reached as a result of engagements through personal experiences and interactions with the surrounding.

2. Genuine Routine

Genuine routines are natural and ritualistic undertakings by the individual. A person engages in a certain routine only as a demonstration of behavioral or habitual ramification of a natural state not because of past exposures to any kind of tendency.

Consider the following scenario to help understand genuine routine:

Scenario 2.8	**Genuine Routine: Natural & Ritualistic (unlearnt tendency) routine**
	Every morning when Josh comes to program, he goes to the bathroom and flicks the lights a couple of times either before using the bathroom or just going in there to flick. Josh also likes walking around the program. He would usually do that by circling the tables and chairs. He does not stop until he completes his runs.

In the above scenario, Josh's behavior is not a result of experience or exposure to bathroom lights or table and chairs. Josh's behavior is ritualistic, and he is insistent on the completion of the steps involve such that they have to be done in a certain way.

An identifying feature of a ritualistic routine is the individual's insistence and commitment to doing and completing a particular task on an ongoing basis. Some behaviors are purely natural and its occurrence is not conditioned on any particular location or under a particular condition.

Scenario 2.9	**Genuine Routine: unlearnt occurrence**
	Danny is an individual who walks more often than she would like to sit throughout the time she is awake. It does not matter where Danny is. Danny only sits for lunch and intermittently between long legs of walking.

The behavior of Danny in *Scenario 2.9* is a genuine natural behavior that occurs not within Danny's control or not as a result of behavior that Danny learnt but a demonstration of her natural state. Danny's act does not stop as long as she is awake.

Sometimes behavior or habit can be harmful to self as well as to others around the individual. A *constellation of tasks* closely related to the habit can help to enhance the impact of the habit on the various facets of the particular routine. However, for harmful or disruptive habit or behavior, a reverse constellation must be used.

a. Reverse constellation

Even when the behavior is not harmful to self or others, it can be alarming in terms of the disruption it causes to the extent that it affects the individual's ability or willingness to engage.

The instances of harmful behavioral routines must be deconstructed by means of *reverse constellation.*

Reverse constellation is the process of replacing the relationship between harmful acts or events that lead to the harmful act with events that will serve a constructive role to the person's overall wellbeing.

Reverse constellation is done by disconnecting sequential events or closely related antecedents that are associated with events that are more likely depict harmful behaviors or sign of a harmful behavior.

Consider the following scenario to help understand how a concerning behavior learnt or resulting from some actions can be reversed:

Scenario 2.10	Reverse Constellation

At the day program, Laura routinely demonstrates the behavior of screaming under the following two conditions: *when her setting (day program) is being noisily saturated and confusing; as well as when she is not getting her choice of certain things at a time she wants it.* What is worth noting about Laura's behavior is that she does not demonstrate those behaviors when she is out of her commonly used setting (such as the day program). Over the years DSPs have generally reported that Laura is very understanding and cooperative when she is out in the community.

Laura's behavior in the community is different from the ones she displays in the day program because in the community, she is alert about her surrounding by the conversations DSP has already had with her prior to the outing as well as prompts the DSP continues giving while in the community. These conversations help Laura to create a mental note of some forms of expectations in the community.

Additionally, Laura gets the attention she craves for without asking for it in the community such that there is really no need to scream for it. In the community DSP ensures that Laura is side by side or at arm's length; DSP keeps reminders and prompts as well as provides necessary cautions; and even physical support when using an escalator or so.

Laura does not get the same level of attention at the day program. For one, there's no stairs or escalator in the program, secondly, she knows the day program layout very much, and there is no requirement of keeping her at arm's length. At program Laura is assisted with preparing her launch, changing in the bathroom, and support with activities directed at her goals of communication and socialization.

Some habits can be meaningful while others might be less meaningful or carried out in a less meaningful manner. Consider the diagram below to understand how Laura's behavior can be deconstructed in order to find a way to curtail concerning ramification.

Breakdown of Laura's behavior at her day program as described in Scenario 2.10. Identifying likely causes of the behavior

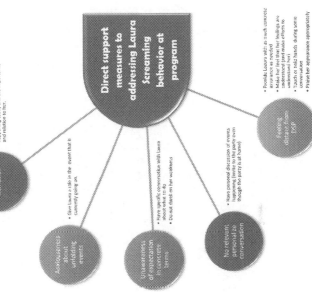

Reasons for Laura screaming behavior at program

- Feeling distant from DSP
  - Fear of being alone
  - Feeling of no understanding or misunderstanding
  - Little to no physical contact
  - nothing to relate

- No relevant personalize conversation
  - Inadequate personal discussion of ongoing events

- Unawareness of expectation in concrete terms
  - Conversation dominated by talks of what not to do

- Anxiousness about unfolding events
  - No appropriate role in any event currently going on.

- Confusion
  - Inadequate personalized clarity

Laura's behavior

Replacing possible triggers with interactions that would make the need for the behavior less likely.

Direct support measures to addressing Laura screaming behavior at program

- Confusion
  - Provide Laura with clarity of what is happening today and the importance and relation to her.

- Anxiousness about unfolding events
  - Give Laura a role in the event that is currently going on.

- Unawareness of expectation in concrete terms
  - Have specific conversation with Laura about what to do
  - Do not dwell on her weakness

- No relevant personalize conversation
  - Have personal discussion of events happening (invite to the party even though the party is at home)

- Feeling distant from DSP
  - Provide Laura with as much concrete assurance as needed
  - Make her feel that her feelings are understood (and make efforts to understand her)
  - Touch or hold hands during some conversation
  - Praise her appearance appropriately

Now that you have an understanding of the individual's DLE by breaking down the instances or steps of the routines and finding the fundamental teachable moments (i.e. opportunity) relevant to a target skill, you will now need to sustain continuous engagement with the individual for two principle reasons: (1) to maintain the understanding and opportunities derived therefrom, and (2) to keep up with any possible developing change of the individual that have the potential to alter your current understanding of the individual's routine.

2. Consistency

The second part of the Opportunity Approach is Consistency. Consistency strengthens the level of understanding regarding a given routine and makes accomplishing an opportunity more likely.

An essential element of maintaining consistency is ensuring that every possible instance of the routine counts. If a routine is identified and assessed for opportunity, DSP will have to closely follow relevant details of the conduct of the routine.

i. Why consistency matters?

Consistency ensures that:

a. The current level of understanding regarding a given routine is monitored and updated.
b. There is continuity and congruity in the effort formulated to support delivery
c. There is coherence within the framework of understanding the individual's routine. Inconsistent engagement slackens the understanding of the individual's routine.
d. There is no fragmented understanding that would obstruct the effort needed to develop enhancement around the routine. Intermittent engagement is less consistent and tends to fragment the understanding into the individual's routine.
    Without consistency, the potential opportunity found within a certain routine cannot be accomplished.

Takeaway—14

Consistency must be a team effort. The specific matter for which consistency is required must be communicated to and known by everyone that works with the person receiving services.

Sometimes the challenges to maintaining consistency lie in the DSP's susceptibility to questioning the meaningfulness of an individual's routine. The meaningfulness of the routine must be judged not from our perspective or the mundaneness of the routine. The meaningfulness must be judged from the perspective of the whole individual and it is usually the function of the individual's physical outlook on the conduct of the routine, the nature of the routine, and the impact of the routine.

The meaningfulness must be judged on the following:

1. Physical outlook on conduct
   a. What moods do the individual display before, during, and after the routine?
   b. Is the mood expressively better than before, during, or after the conduct of the routine?
2. Nature of the routine
   a. Is the routine natural (Genuine) or learnt (Artificial)?
   b. Is the routine an escape from some other events, or a transition to an event?
3. Impact
   a. What is the impact on self and on others?
      i. Is it harmful to self or others? If not harmful, is it disruptive to the affairs of self or others

Although sometimes difficult to ascertain, answers to the questions above will be able to indicate whether the individual appreciates the occurrence and derives happiness from it or the routine is such that the individual only engages in it because of uncontrollable factors that are part and parcel or likely features of a given diagnosis.

Importantly, a routine does not necessarily have to make sense to a DSP before it can be explored. For instance, when smoking is someone else's routine (habit), we don't necessarily have to believe in smoking in order to be considerate towards the smoker. We have to respect the person's choice of smoking. If smoking is suspected of being specifically harmful to the particular person, clinical or medical referral should be made; and based on findings of the referrals, the relevant supports can be provided. In the same vein, as shown in Scenario 2.8 one does not have to believe in Josh's habit of walking around chairs and table before Josh can receive the necessary accommodation he deserves.

ii.   Frequency of the routine

The frequency of the routine is the span of the routine. The frequency of the routine helps us to understand the regularity at which the routine occurs. The frequency can either be *transit* or *tunnel*.

1.   *Transit Routines* are short routines. They are routines *in passage* and they are usually the individual's way of transitioning.

Consider the below scenario to understand how a routine in passage is a way of transitioning for the individual conducting it:

> **Scenario 2.11   Transit Routines**
>
> Jenny walks to certain staff in the morning and tell the staff the date, time, and present or nearest holiday. Jenny does not do this for the entire day only at a particular time of the day and once she does it in the morning, she does not go back to it for the rest of that day. But it is such that Jenny must complete that cycle before she can be able to satisfactorily embark on any other tasks.

2.   *Tunnel Routine* is a lengthier interaction on the part of the individual. Often Tunnel routines tend to be final activities of the individual. Individuals that are involved with tunnel routine usually do all of the things they have to do and then retire to the tunnel routine. Other times, they are not even willing to do anything other than the tunnel routine.

Individuals engaging in tunnel routine rarely normally desist by themselves. However, depending on individual characteristics, some do respond to prompts and redirection based on the individual's preference of interactions.

Redirection can be a way of introducing new options or exposure of the individual to some similar and possible alternatives. Redirection an also include inserting other actions within the individual's routine by breaking the routine into segments.

Scenario 2.12	Tunnel Routines
Mat sits and watches wrestling videos on his iPad for more than 2 to 3 strict hours. He pauses, uses the restroom and comes back to it.	

Understanding the frequency of the routine can make possible its incorporation into other activities directed at other areas of preference that the individual is working on. In the above scenario, Mat's tunnel routine can be broken down in order to find out what part of the routine can be an opportunity to explore and develop further.

Giving the routine all of the attention and consideration it deserves is the beginning. DSP must breakdown the routine so as to enumerate the skills and willingness exhibited into conducting it. See Diagram 4 for how to accomplish this.

When important instances such as those occurring in tunnel and transit routines are not timely and appropriately explored, a *Missed Opportunity* results.

a. *Missed opportunity* occurs when there is a lack of consistency in exploring and engaging the individual in their routines.

Scenario 2.13 **Missed Opportunity**

Consider the facts presented earlier that Mat sits and watches wrestling videos on his iPad for more than 2 to 3 strict hours. He pauses, uses the restroom and comes back to it. If Mat is left by himself to continue with the routine without taking advantage of the willingness and skills he puts into the iPad routine, the DSP will be missing on potential opportunities that could have otherwise been explored and incorporated into Mat's overall goals.

---

iii. Incorporating Routine and Goal

Both transit and runnel routines can be incorporated into the relevant activity by taking advantage of the timing and span of the individual routine. Consider Scenario 2.11 where Jenny's self-initiated engagement with the DSP is a better opportunity to start talking to Jenny about a range of things that are related to her goal and other preferences. Jenny's contact with the DSP is a circumstance (i.e. a potential opportunity) that the DSP can accomplished into an opportunity if the right kind of engagement is reciprocated by the DSP overtime in a consistent manner.

Since it is certain that once Jenny comes to program she will have to engage with certain DSPs, the particular DSP can reciprocate Jenny's contact and make attempt at expanding the conversation to areas for which Jenny has a set goal. This way the DSP is incorporating element of the goal within Jenny's routine if it is not already a written part of Jenny's habilitation plan. However, ideally, goals must have already been set based on Jenny's routine and not the routine based on the goal.

Similar strategy applies to Scenario 2.12 in which Mat is fond of a Tunnel routine of sitting and watching wrestling videos on his iPad for a considerable time at the day program. One way of incorporating Mat's goal into his long routine is to insert his goal activities into the use of the iPad and time the routine into segments so that the goal related activity can supplement the continuation of the routine.

For instance, if Mat is working on socialization and communication goals specifically related to him attaining the skills at expressing himself verbally instead of displaying behaviors that pose danger both to himself and others around him, there are the Conover Functional Skills System iPad applications for both of Mat's goals. Those applications can be apportioned as a part of Mat's routine with support from DSP.

The irony here is that the routine should supplement the goal since in fact it is the goal that is more compliant related.

1. Branching out

It is less challenging when the current goals are already formed around the central components of the routine that the individual willingly engages in. That way the individual's conduct of the routine will also mean working on parts of the goal with the appropriate support from DSP.

The individual's routine can be branched out gradually by exposure to new experiences that introduces the individual to additional resources to help make additional preferences.

Consider the following scenario to help understand how a routine can be branched out

Scenario 2.13	Branching out

Maria is an individual receiving services; she is independent in a range of daily living activities. Maria has employment experience and has a very good potential of future employment. Maria engages in a number Transit Routines at different times of the day. She is an independent travel so comes to program by herself. In the morning at program, she would take the phone from night mode to day mode and would usually answer calls coming between the 8:30AM to 9AM. At 9AM she would announce on the paging system that it was time for arrival as soon as the transportation buses come in. Then at about 3PM, she would take the phone to also announce that it was time for dismissal.

These routines are short routines, however, the skills involve in conducting them can be bifurcated into necessary skills directed at completing other goals that will be more rewarding to Maria.

The skills involved in switching the phone from night to day mode, and answering and transferring calls can be used to complete part of a receptionist task, for instance. Based on these routines, Maria can be exposed to the possibility of serving as a receptionist or any other task where those skills can be applied. Maria may or may not make the choice by herself if she is not expose to as many possibilities as there are that her skills can get her.

Branching out is the process of using the individual's routine to derive a goal where the skills used to complete the routine are the same as the ones required for the goals.

The following Venn diagram explains the process of branching out more clearly:

Diagram 11: Branching out the routine

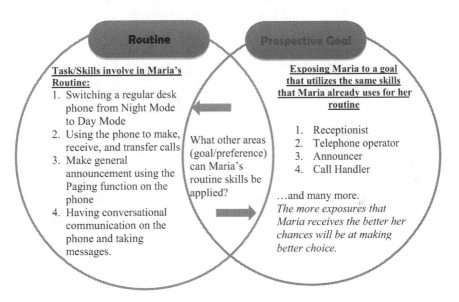

Routine

Prospective Goal

<u>Task/Skills involve in Maria's Routine:</u>
1. Switching a regular desk phone from Night Mode to Day Mode
2. Using the phone to make, receive, and transfer calls
3. Make general announcement using the Paging function on the phone
4. Having conversational communication on the phone and taking messages.

What other areas (goal/preference) can Maria's routine skills be applied?

<u>Exposing Maria to a goal that utilizes the same skills that Maria already uses for her routine</u>

1. Receptionist
2. Telephone operator
3. Announcer
4. Call Handler

…and many more.
The more exposures that Maria receives the better her chances will be at making better choice.

    a.   Opportunity Leads (OL)

Other times the nature of the routine poses practical challenges to branching it out into some other goals. Consider Scenario 2.8 discussed earlier where the individual flicks the bathroom lights on and off, and does a walkthrough between table and chairs before settling down at his table and determine what can DSP and the individual receiving services do to benefit more from these routines?

Opportunity leads are exposures through the creation of baits in the form of clues, hints, and trials of activities that are presented to the individual in a less structure and informal manner.

The more regularly the individual is shown to activities related to an exposure the more he/she will be likely to pick up the patterns. Leads are helpful in obtaining an individual's attention especially for the personality of individuals who respond unfavorably to direction or facilitation. Leads can be in the form of *Soft Contacts* such as communication about new and exciting possibilities as well as physical interaction with other opportunities.

iv. Making consistency work

Often DSPs do brilliant jobs at supporting the people receiving services. They put their minds and hearts into the helping relationship and gain the affection and trust of the persons being served which helps in effecting enhancement within the individual's target skills. However, over and over again, DSP see very little fruit out of the efforts they put into the process of direct support. Most DSPs have mastery at finding the teachable moments (i.e. opportunity) in the everyday interactions (i.e. routine) of the individuals but every so often they do not reach their own goals of helping the persons receiving services reach their individual goals.

Takeaway—14

Regardless how skillful a DSP is at breaking down the individual's routine or behavior, and regardless of how many innovative ideas there is to be applied to those breakdowns, the key components of reaching a goal is to maintain consistency both in assessing one's own understanding of the individual's routines and in the utilization of the opportunities presented by the individual's routines..

The following are ways to maintain consistency:

i. *Adequate understanding about the issues*: There must be sufficient facts about the matter that requires uniform processing. The team of managers and DSPs involve with the individual must know what is going on and why consistency is critical to the particular issue at hand. Adequate understanding also means that all the pieces of shared information are updated timely. Adequate understanding about the issue also includes providing the requisite training so as to ensure that the issues or situations are understood by those involve in its implementation.

ii. *Conformity of system guiding continuity:* Any measures put in place to ensure consistency must be followed by everyone involved with providing service to the individual. In essence, there should be only one way of dealing with the particular issue. If any other ways of dealing with the issue has been uncover, it should be put to the team or a designated person to work out the details to ensure that it becomes the only uniform way of guiding continuity toward the goal of consistency. Every team member must be required to handle and respond to the identified issue in the same format.

iii. *Availability of necessary resources:* Every tool required for informing and maintaining consistency must be available to those charged with ensuring consistency. These includes service plans, evaluations, and any other materials that will inform and make the process of continuity possible and sustainable.

iv. *Patience*: Life is full of numerous phenomena that do not happen the way we plan for it or at the time we anticipate it. Disappointment or motivation killer moments come your way very often than not yet still there is perseverance to see through to the end. The effort to see the person receiving service improve their skills and overall affairs in activities of daily living and community relations is rarely possible when the source of direct support lacks persistence and endurance. Often times, frustration results after numerous honest efforts directed at improving the helping relationship fail to meet our expectations.

Very often than not our impatience is misdirected at the individual receiving services than at ourselves. We set expectations for ourselves for what we want the individual to achieve instead of setting realistic expectations from the perspective of the individual. DSPs should guide their impatience so as to avoid undue frustration. When misdirected impatience ensues, frustration results and sometimes to either avoid frustration or as a way of dealing with it, we recommend new ways of dealing with the given issues even when current approach has not been adequately exhausted.

v. *Acknowledgement*: DSP and the individuals alike need feedback regarding the level of steadiness and regularity exhibited toward a particular issue. No matter how meaningful the consistency is intended to be beneficial, the individual ironically had to forego some other things in order to stay guided on a specific track. Likewise, if for one thing, the DSP will have to forego any easier and less guided way of doing things only to maintain consistency required to support the individual achieve a target goal.

DSP and individual involve with the subject of consistency must be acknowledged and commended as frequently as possible. This will cultivate the feeling that their work is being monitored, their patience well held, and their progress appreciated.

Diagram 12: Consistency in Direct Support

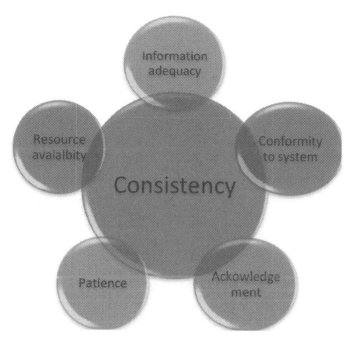

The Opportunity Approach is effectively applied when a goal has been achieved as a result. Now, with the understanding of the DLE and consistency at working with the various parts of the routine, eyes must always be kept on the final and bigger picture—the goal.

3. Goal Attainment

The third element of the Opportunity Approach is goal attainment or maintenance. A group day habilitation goal is the object towards which support services are directed. The goal is reached and nurtured through the direct support process. However the process of direct support is such that it is unlike most other processes because there is no finished product. There are usually milestones that are themselves not independently useful except used to achieve some other supplementary milestones and so on.

Goals differ from person to person. To determine what goal to adopt or to help the individual to make preferences in order to derive a goal, exploration new experiences is usually the way of making discovery and formation of new preferences more likely. Exploration must be refined and targeted in order to be effective. One way to refine an exploration with the individual is to narrow down the concentration of the interaction to specific goals.

Goals are usually set in order to maintain current skill, *or* attain new skills evolved as result of new exposures and experiences.

    i.   Maintenance of current skills

Maintaining current skills means that the individual's existing skill will continue to receive needed support or support is directed at maintaining the effort involved with nurturing an emerging skill.

If a goal is specifically adopted to maintain a current skill, action directed at the goal is generally dispensed as a way of providing the individual additional supports to enhance the individual existing capabilities for which the DSP must keep up with the individual's routine by:

    a)   Demonstrating appreciation for the routine that is the target of the staff action. What this means is that DSP must show recognition, admiration, and demonstrate full understanding of the individual's situation and efforts in the routine. "Diagram 4: Breakdown of the routine" is an effect way to start to understand the individual's routine. Working to maintain the existing skill is only possible when the DSP is consistent in the process however, the first step forward is for the DSP to exhibit empathy and appreciation of the individual's involvement.

    b)   Understanding the preference and its task constellation: The task constellation is the connected activities or all of the tasks that make up a preference. See Diagram 9 for more detail. Through the understanding of the task DSP can create the circumstance, stimulation, and facilitation needed to nurture the current skill.

c) Considering how the routine is related to the other activities in a given constellation: Understanding the role of the routine in the individual's overall wellbeing is essential to such understanding. DSP must ensure to make relationship with the routine because it is from the conduct of the routine that most hidden but existing skills are discovered as well.

D

Scenarios of opportunity

There are three opportunity scenarios: Time, Environment, and Special Occurrence/Event

1. *Opportunity Time:* An opportunity time is the particular interval at which a given routine occurs or at which it is most likely to occur. It refers to both the chronological timetable, and the instances or sequence of the occurrence.

    Consider the following scenario to help understand opportunity time:

Scenario 2.14	Opportunity Time
Jim tells the weather of the following day at about before dismissal time. Hence, briefly engaging Jim at about this time with activities in the weather constellation is more likely to help to expand Jim's horizons of this routine. An opportunity exists when the time surrounding Jim's routine is effectively utilized.	

The above scenario is basically placing emphasis on initiating a support at the time when it is most contextually relevant.

2. *Opportunity Environment:* An opportunity environment is the specific venue in which a particular routine is most likely to occur.

Scenario 2.15	Opportunity Environment
Pat does not sing at the day program however, she sings whenever she is at a mall.	
Pat would gather a crowd when she starts to sing. She sings songs from the 70's in very classic fashion and skips from one oldies to the next. The scene can be so powerful that people would stop to listen in reminiscence of the past.	

For the most part, mall locations bring out the musician in Pat and as such locations like those present the best opportunity to engage Pat in things that are related to her goal and preference.

> i. *Group Environment:* Some individuals display a certain routine when in a group that they would not otherwise carry out when they are engaged on an individual level.
>
> Activities related to any such routine motivated by group participation must be put into constellation in order to export the necessary components from the group setting to other relevant areas of the individual's overall support framework.
>
> ii. *Individual Environment:* Similarly, an individual may likely demonstrate certain routine by herself without the influence of a group and in fact may only carry out a certain routine by herself or when engaged individually. Customized efforts should be applied in ensuring that the individual is supported in making the most out of both individual and group environments.

3. *Special Occurrence Opportunity:* A special occurrence exists where certain routines (especially Transit Routines) are initiated based on a particular unfolding event, condition, or the presence of a particular person.

   Consider the following scenario to help understand opportunity occurring during special events:

Scenario 2.16	Special Occurrence Opportunity

Van Y is a senior and so he and other seniors from the day program sometimes visit a nearby senior center. Van Y is usually quiet and although he communicates fairly verbally, he would prefer to respond to DSP in one to two words.

The senior center that he frequents usually hosts birthday parties for their seniors once every month. When Van Y is invited to those monthly parties, he blushes as he dances with senior females to songs that he could be heard singing.

In the above scenario, Van Y engages in those routines only during the special occasion at the senior center. To better support Van Y, DSP must make consistent effort at exposing Van Y to further experiences especially to those similar to those in the senior center.

Understanding a routine of the individual in relation to the time of occurrence, the environment, and special circumstances surrounding the initiation and conduct of the routine provides one of the most effective tools to making an *Opportunity* out of the instances of a routine.

E

Challenges to Opportunity Approach

Direct support is dynamic and intricate, and there is no any known source that addresses direct support issues with a single tool. Like any current tool in the field, OA has its own challenges some of which are summarized below:

➤ Unpredictable Behavioral challenges

 A perfect example of this is a change in medication that have adverse physical effects on the individual. As stated earlier in this chapter, a routine or behavior must be anticipated in order for it to be applied to a constellation or reverse constellation that would be needed to address any known behavioral routine challenges or opportunities. If the behavior or a certain act is unpredictable it becomes hard to effectively navigate.

➤ Extreme inability to focus

 An individual's extreme inability to focus can defy the techniques and prospects of contacts and engagement both of which are critically essential parts of OA.

➤ DSP's failure to make meaning of, understand or appreciate the routine.

 Overlooking or overemphasizing events of the individual's routine

➤ Clustering (i.e. weaving important but unrelated instances of routines)

 Too distant from routine in the constellation

➤ Inconsistency

There is always opportunity to explore regarding the individual. A lack of opportunity means that the individual has no past, present or developing preferences which is rarely a possibility.

F

Chapter Summary

1. If a given staff action is missing any one of the features of NAMO that staff action is more likely to fall short of meeting the individual target skills. The reality of the staff action must always be a unique reflection of actions that the individual can undertake independently or has the capability to act on when the appropriate support is provided.

2. An opportunity in the staff action means that the particular staff action creates the circumstance, stimulation, and facilitation necessary for the application of the service delivery methodology.

3. The Circumstance is the event or action similar to those in which the target skill will more likely occur. Stimulation is a non-coercive and aversive trigger that cultivates interest in the circumstance created while Facilitation is the efforts that is enabling and necessary for utilizing the circumstance more effectively.

4. DSP must break down an individual's DLE into the specific steps require to complete an entire process or into steps necessary to complete part of the process that reflects the individual's capability and level of functioning into consideration.

5. Consistency must be a team effort. The specific matter for which consistency is required must be communicated to and known by everyone that works with the person receiving services.

6. Regardless how skillful a DSP is at breaking down the individual's routine or behavior, and regardless of how many innovative ideas there is to be applied to those breakdowns, the key components of reaching a goal is to maintain consistency both in assessing

one's own understanding of the individual's routines and in the utilization of the opportunities presented by the routines.

There is always opportunity to explore regarding the individual. A lack of opportunity means that the individual has no past, present or developing preferences.

3

chapter

Assessing Discovery

Furthering staff action

OBJECTIVE OF THIS CHAPTER

By the end of this chapter, you will be able to demonstrate:

1. Knowledge of how to enhance staff action through exposure and discovery
2. Understanding of the types and categories of discovery
3. Knowledge of the characteristics of responses and techniques of how to improve them

A

Discovery: Furthering staff action

Discovery and direct support are two features of day habilitation that go hand in hand. Discovery furthers direct support by challenging the staff action into finding new perspectives of dealing with an individual's evolving realities. Staff action, on the other hand, is based on previously discovered or evolving information about the individual and is designed to produce even more discoveries in order to be considered an effective process.

Consider the following scenario to help understand discovery and direct support relationship:

Scenario 3.1	*Discovery and Staff Action*

Amy is currently pursuing a goal of becoming a waitress. She is being exposed to volunteering at two community centers three days a week. She goes to a senior center two times a week and to a church outreach program once a week. The different locations afford Amy to diversify her experience of volunteering. This preference was discovered in a recent meeting when Amy's mother stated that Amy has always wanted to be a waitress, and that she loves serving people so much that she serves dinner at home on most evenings. Amy confirmed and stated that serving as a waitress is something she would like to do. Since Amy began volunteering, her relationship with people have improved essentially and socially appropriate. She has also learnt to serve food to the right table, and staying at arm's length when asking people if they enjoy the food and whether they would like any assistance. Often, she tells community members to come back and to tell their friends of the location.

These were all breakthroughs (*i.e. discovery*) for Amy as she did not know what to do or say or how to stay appropriate when she started volunteering couple of weeks earlier. Based on these breakthroughs, the direct support process through the DSP was now challenged to find new ways of utilizing Amy's new found skills.

Diagram # 13: Direct Discovery & Staff Action

Consider the diagram below to further explain the scenario above:

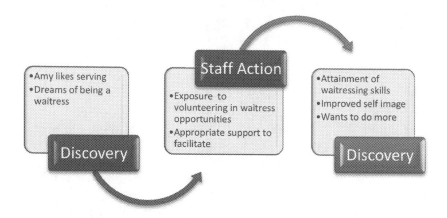

As you noticed from the above scenario, a discovery led to a particular staff action, and the staff action was effective in helping Amy learn new skills which now had to be appropriately utilized so that Amy can gain much more.

Takeaway—19

DSP must constantly observe for outcomes of and reaction to support being provided during direct engagement with the individual. The ongoing process of discovery is a form of nonclinical assessment that informs and widens the supports mechanism for the individual; and suggests data that are relevant to maintaining or modifying current care plan.

B

Types of Discovery

Discovery in direct support is an ongoing lifelong process that is usually encountered through:

- Technical Discovery which refers to developments that shift the overall policies and approaches to service types and delivery at agency, local, state, and federal levels;
- Direct Discovery which is basically direct interaction with individuals receiving services including consistent exposures to new experiences.

1. Technical Discovery

Technical discovery refers to the kinds of discoveries that are clinical or those discoveries that are not immediate results of direct staff actions. Technical discovery often serves to inform the direct support process and guides staff actions into the direction of the prevailing policy. Technical discovery include any other process that provides information about the field through means other than the direct support process. It includes clinical evaluations, scientific journals, journalist reporting, agency and industry policies, as well as governmental guidelines regarding the population and the services provided.

Technical discovery offers a system of evolving knowledge building upon existing information about things— things that were not known up to the time of the discovery. Technical discoveries are information about the field and

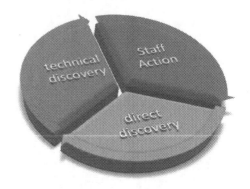

services that individuals receive as well as updates to the existing system of knowledge and operations.

As depicted in the diagram below, *technical discovery* informs *staff action* in the forms of policies, scientific findings, and field policies describing allowable procedures, treatment or service types as well as what kind of staff action will be consider empowering or otherwise. Consider the following scenario to help understand technical discovery:

Scenario 3.2	*Technical discovery*

Recently New York State setup the New York Justice Center to protect people with intellectual and developmental disabilities from abuse, neglect and mistreatment.

The 2014 Federal Home and Community-Based Services Regulation by CMS now defines institutions as "any other setting that has the effect of isolating individuals receiving Medicaid HCBS from the broader community of individuals not receiving Medicaid HCBS." . . . and that "Congregate settings may be included (as home and community-based settings) if they meet the HCB setting requirements set forth in this rule."[2]

The CMS preamble also states that "Individuals must be afforded choice regarding the activities in which they wish to participate including whether to participate in a group activity or to engage in other activities which may not be pre-planned."

Service providers integrate these policy guidelines into internal system of delivery that are usually reflected in direct support staff actions.

---

[2]   "The 2014 Federal Home and Community-Based . . . - The Arc." 2014. 19 Apr. 2014 <http://www.thearc.org/document.doc?id=4596>

Diagram # 15: Technical Discovery & Staff Action

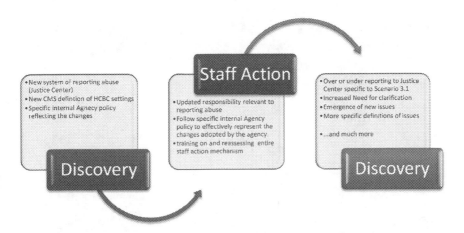

Diagram #15 explains Scenario 3.2 in terms of the describing the impact and role that technical discovery plays in effecting generic shift in staff action into reflecting the trend in the field.

2. Direct Discovery

Direct discovery is the second type of discovery that is more specific in modeling staff action based on individualized information and unique individual responses to a given staff action.

Direct discovery results from the individual's response to staff action including exposure to new experiences. For the purpose of our discussion on discovery, this chapter will mainly be focused on *direct discovery*.

Direct discovery is ever evolving and it is based on individualized support to and personalized responses from individuals. Direct discovery is more fluid and it furthers the practical process of direct support. Scenario 3.1 and Diagram #13 are examples of direct discovery.

A detailed discussion of direct discovery requires an understanding into the characteristics of responses and the categories of direct discovery that cover them.

Before diving into the discussion of understanding direct discovery, consider referring to the below diagram as we cover each component of the direct discovery:

Diagram # 16: Understanding Direct Discovery

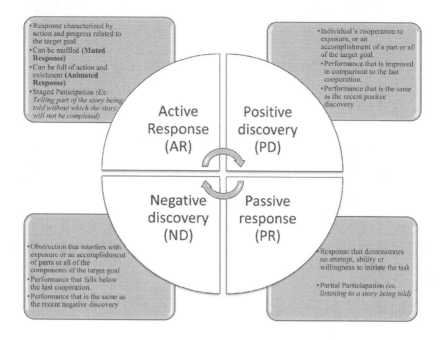

Each component of the above matrix is discussed below:

> i.   Characteristics of responses

At any given time during the application of a staff action, an individual will either be receptive or unreceptive, and will usually do so by demonstrating *passive or active response* relevant to the level of reception to the staff action.

> 1.   Passive Response

An individual demonstrates passive response by doing nothing more than being available at the target event or does nothing during a demonstration of a staff action without any attempt, willingness, or ability to initiate the task.

✓   A response is passive when the individual is merely accepting direction or facilitation without the willingness or ability to complete the task even when presented with the same set of tools and opportunity.

Scenario 3.3   *Passive Response*

Evelyn was accompanied to the nearby local community library as part of a planned community trip for the purpose of attending a personal storytelling event moderated by the head librarian. She was taken to the event by the DSP even though she was not supported in preparation for the storytelling event or commutation in general. Evelyn only sat in at the event and listened while the DSP told Evelyn's story from what he knew of Evelyn as far as socialization was concern.

In the scenario above, Evelyn partially participated in the session by being present and listening in. Although actions were required on Evelyn's part, she did not attempt to do anything and could not do anything as far as capability and preference were concern or probably because the DSP did not prepare Evelyn enough for the event. Evelyn's response was *passive*.

An extensive passive response can encourage a sense of dependency whereby the individual looks to the DSP or active peers as the authority figure who can be relied upon for the completion of the task.

Takeaway—20

When passive response becomes a routine it causes stagnation in the individual prospects and willingness to personally attempt initiating the task.

    a.   Causes of Passive Responses

         i.   Passive response can result from a past experience that either did not receive appropriate feedback or commendation or the individual did not appreciate the initial experience with the events out of personal disinterest.

            Past events play a formidable role in the daily routines of individuals with developmental and intellectual disabilities. Most of the routines themselves are based on preferences formed from experiences with tasks, events or behaviors that were encountered at some times in the past.

ii. It can also be a result of the individual's involvement in a task or event that is not properly understood by the individual.

iii. Passive response also comes about when the event is too distant from the individual's routine such that the conduct of it poses practical challenges to the individual's existing ability.

The distance between a routine and a new event is the lack of virtual connection between the two or where both the routine and the new event share no skills required for the completion of the other.

Consider the following scenario to explain this distance in virtual connection:

Scenario 3.4   *Distance between routine and new events (preference)*

Marley is working on a routine that involves using a visual guide to only sort out spoon, fork and knife designed around Marley's capability. Now, Marley expresses a preference for a volunteer opportunity involving answering phones.

Marley's current routine is distant from his new expressed preference. The virtual distance can be reduced by either expanding on the routine or narrowing down the new preference so that it can be met gradually within the scope of the skills used by Marley to carry out the routine. Marley's routine at the day program can be expanded by introducing related tasks so that the skills gained from the routine are utilized under circumstances similar to the new preference.

For instance, Marley can be exposed to volunteering in sorting out spoon, fork, and knife in the soup kitchen; and even if Marley cannot participate wholly, the task can be portioned in a divided arrangement where he is tasked with all or divided portion of the task. Gradually a volunteering opportunity in a soup kitchen which involves taking orders may develop, among other things, Marley's interpersonal skills and improve communication skills that could be transferred to the skills required for answering phones (since in fact answering phone involves interactive communication with people as well).

Distance, in this instance, means the lack of relationship between Marley's present routine and the developing events especially where the two tasks share no skills in common requires for the completion of either event.

b. Improving Passive Responses

When a passive response is determined to be the result of the individual's experience with similar events in the past, DSP must provide assurance directed at how the current encounter will be different, and why the current encounter will be different.

Consider the following scenario to understand how passive responses can be improved:

Scenario 3.5	*Dealing with passive response resulting from past experience*

Marisol attended a musical event at Bryant Park on 42nd Street a couple of weeks ago. She was scheduled for a short performance for which she had practiced well enough. She came to program appropriately dressed for the occasion. However, Marisol and her DSP did not get to the performance in time thus causing Marisol to forfeit her slot for performance. DSP tried negotiating with the organizers to find another slot for Marisol's performance but none was available. Marisol returned to program devastated.

A month later, the DSP found another opportunity for Marisol, explained the details to her, and asked her if she would like to perform at the event. Marisol shook her head in decline. A few days later, DSP approached Marisol again with the idea. DSP provided concrete assurance that a program vehicle has been allocated to drop them off at the event; that her performance has been scheduled an hour later than the first event, and that they would be leaving a little earlier so that they could see part of the event before Marisol's performance. DSP also described to Marisol the event and some of the other performance that were expected.

DSP needs to be aware of the relationship between the *present* (which is the routine) and the *future* (which is the goal that the individual will be upon the performance of the task being introduced).

i. Staged Participation

Staged participation is the arrangement whereby the event or task is divided amongst the people working to complete it. Staging the participation must be accompanied by communication about the need to complete the task and why the individual's role in the process is important.

In scenario 3.4, DSP can structure the individual participation into a *staged participation* wherein the individual will have a part to play as part of the completion of the event.

Consider the following scenario to help understand Staged Participation:

Scenario 3.6   *Staged Participation*

DSP engaged Flora and friends if they were interested in making fruit salad. Flora and friends named the fruits to purchase as the DSP write it down. DSP accompanied them to the nearby supermarket where the fruits were purchased.

The salad were to consist of six different fruits. Flora and her two friends were assigned two fruits each to open the facet to the appropriate temperature and wash their respective fruits. Each of them was require to fetch a bowl from the kitchen and place their fruits in. DSP called upon each pair of fruits and each of the individual was to slice their fruits with DSP's guidance. In order to complete the six-fruit salad, all of the participants will have to work on completing their parts of the task.

Participation of each of the individuals in the above scenario is staged so that it is completed together in full. The six-fruit salad could not have been possible without the completion of assigned portion of the overall fruit salad task.

Diagram #17: Partial Participation

Diagram #18: Staged Participation

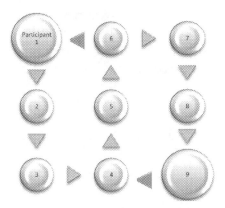

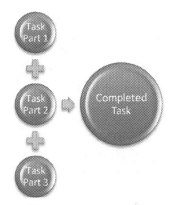

A perfect example of Partial Participation is a scenario where a DSP tells a story while the participants only listen either because they are unwilling to take part, or they don't understand the subject at hand, or because their capability is challenged by the skills require by the task. Partial participation is passive.

Consider the same storytelling example but only that this case is a Staged Participation. In Staged Participation, the participants actively take part in completing the task wherein the absence of one part affects the whole such that if Part 1 of the story is not told parts 2 and 3 will not make a complete whole of the story.

Takeaway—21

Partial participation does not require any role on the part of the individual other than being present with the exception of where the sole performance of the task only require the presence of the individual. In a staged participation, the individual is actually performing actively toward the completion of the task. Participation under staged structure is important from each individual to ensure that the task reaches its stated goal.

Irrespective of the type of participation that the individual is involved with, DSP must make effort to invoke the individual's consciousness into the matter at hand by having timely and specific conversations about the project; why the individual's participation in the project is crucial to completing the project; as well as furnishing the individual with all the tools and facilitation needed to initiate participation and completion of the event or task.

Depending on the individual being supported such invocation might not be necessary given the unique characteristics of the impairing challenges.

2. Active Response

An active response arises when an individual reacts to staff action in a way that is characterized by action and progress related to the given goal. *Staged participation* is form an active response.

Under an active response, reactions can be either muted or animated:

a. Muted response

A muted reaction is a suppressed response depicted as a result of some unfolding situations obstructing the individual's active involvement.

A mute reaction occurs wherein the individual is neither *passive* nor completely *active*. Consider the following scenario to understand a muted reaction:

Scenario 3.7   *Active Response—Mute Reaction*
Jenny loves making patterned beads necklace and has been producing beautiful necklaces. Yesterday, she made a beautiful one that she took home for her mom. But today, Jenny is sitting at the table with the necklace making materials in front of her but she is not completely active with the activity. Usually, she completes a necklace in two hours but now she has only put three pieces of beads on the wire in 1½ hours.

In the above scenario, Jenny's reaction is muffled or refrained from being expressive even though the event at hand is one derived based on Jenny's preference and capability. In this case, Jenny is not completely active as compare to Jenny's history with the same event but she is not passive either because she is able to attempt or initiate the particular event independently beyond mere presence.

Takeaway—22

Emotional, medical, and structural changes are the most common factors that contribute to a mute reaction.

Change in staff, tempered interaction from home or changes affecting relationship with peers or significant others can impact the emotions and affect the manner in which the individual react to direct support.

Changes in the structure of the operation of things including a routine may be unsettling from the onset of such change and are more likely to disrupt the flow of the individual's interactions and subsequent reactions to staff action.

---

i.   Unmuting the response

Communicating with the individual to understand how she feels, as well as external communication with families or other service providers is an essential step toward unlocking understanding into the emotions at any given time.

The following two steps can be used to unmute an individual reaction:

a.   A reaction can be unmuted by creating a sense of empathy that demonstrates the DSP's awareness of the individual's emotional state.

b.   Make connection with the individual existing connection to understand any underlying and contributing factor to the individual's current state. Communication is critical throughout direct engagement but especially in understanding the current emotional state of the individual.

An extended muted reaction to staff action is a genuine reason to revisit the direct support process including staff action.

b. Animated Reaction

The second part of the active response is the animated reaction. An animated reaction is an active response that is characterized by progress and spirited expression exemplifying awareness of both the event at hand and the surrounding in which it is taking place.

Scenario 3.8   *Active Response—Animated Reaction*

Al is a semi-verbal individual who does not speak often but when he talks he does so in one word or nodding in approval or disapproval. Al is being supported in the areas of improving his knowledge and skills of sign language. Al has been working with this area for about a year now. But this week, from Monday to Thursday Al has been observed signing all of the six words that he is working on—lunch, bathroom, drink, more, please, and thank you. Usually when the DSP signs, Al would not respond instead he would just proceed in the direction of what he wants to do such like going to the kitchen for lunch or to drink instead of signing them, or going toward the bathroom to use the toilet. For today specifically, he signed some of the words as well as responded to the DSP when the DSP signed some of his words to him (Al).

Al response in the above scenario is an animated response considering the exemplification of awareness of the context and action.

ii. Recording Direct Discovery:

As stated earlier, direct discovery is a product of an individual's response to exposure to new experiences as well as the individual's riposte to the specific staff action directed at a target goal.

So if a DSP exposes an individual to some new community outings or support the individual through other actions intended to help with goal attainment or maintenance, in what category of responses should the individual's response be recorded?

There are two categories in which direct discovery can be recorded. They are positive and negative discoveries:

1. Positive discovery arises out of the individual's cooperation with staff actions directed at supporting the individual toward a skill, or out of the individual's accomplishment of parts or all of the components of the target goal.

Consider the following scenario to help understand positive discovery:

Scenario 3.9   *Positive Discovery*

Mark is being supported in the areas of improving his communications by learning to sign "please" and "thank you". Mark likes coffee and it is one of the things that he would not want to go without. Today he took an unused coffee cup and sign "please" to the DSP who was amused by Mark's inclination. DSP accompanied Mark to the kitchen and prepared a cup of coffee along with Mark. DSP served Mark with the coffee and for a moment Mark didn't sign "thank you." DSP appropriately prompt Mark a few moments later to always sign "thank you" whenever someone does something for him. Mark didn't respond until they left the kitchen and went back to their table. Mark placed the cup of coffee on the table and signed "Thank you" to the DSP. DSP was very excited about Mark's ability to learn from the support.

Events in the above scenario could be term as an accomplishment based on past responses from Mark. If Mark had only signed one of the two at every other time in the past, the above scenario can be considered an accomplishment. To understand positive discovery and characteristics of response, refer to *Diagram # 16: Understanding Direct Discovery*.

A positive discovery supposes that the method of the direct supports is being effective in arising the desired reaction or outcome from the individual being supported.

Sometimes a discovery can be positive even though there is no upward movement within the individual's goal in terms of accomplishment. Cooperation can be a discovery when it has been achieved in relation to the individual's last response to the same staff action and under the same circumstances

Consider the following scenario to help understand how cooperation can be a discovery:

Scenario 3.10	*Cooperation as a positive discovery*

Rob is pursuing a valued outcome of learning to do light janitorial work at a community center where he is accompanied by DSP. He is learning how to replace garbage bags, and learning to say excuse me to workers in the cubicles before reaching for the garbage bins. Now Rob's reaction is such that he knows how to do the task but still requires the same amount of prompts about the sequence and reminders to use appropriate tone of voice in that office area. So while Rob can do the actual task he is not comfortable enough to move to any other steps. Rob is doing the same thing sometimes correctly but most times incorrectly, hence, the need for DSP support has not changed in anyway. Rob's current response to the DSP action is that he diligently follows the steps required in completing the task and is working together with the support process very well.

In the above scenario, Rob's cooperation to the support being provided is positive as compare to the previous response where he would argue and insist on knowing what to do when he was actually making errors. Also, when an individual's reaction to the direct support is such that the individual has maintained a goal without regression, the discovery will be that but for the method of direct support the individual has maintained the goal set and embraced by the team including the individual. Such is a discovery that is positive because if it weren't for the method of direct support the individual would have regressed.

To maintain a positive discovery, the staff action must contain the NAMO features discussed in Chapter 2.

2. Negative Discovery

The second category of direct discovery is negative discovery:

a. A negative discovery occurs when unexpected reactions obstruct successful application of the staff action or causes unfavorable responses that does not advance the staff action in any way.

Consider the following scenario to understand reactions that obstructs or impedes progress of a staff action:

Scenario 3.11   *Negative discovery—unexpected reaction*

Sergey has been involved with a routine of photography in which he and his friend Boris would go with DSP and take pictures of beautiful sceneries and other interesting things. Sergey has been using basic Adobe Photoshop functionalities to enhance his pictures with facilitation from DSP.

In a separate experience while at home, Sergey was watching TV when he saw a paparazzi's camera was smashed down by someone who didn't want to be photographed. The paparazzi was almost hit as well and the camera was damaged.

On the next day at program Sergey was supposed to go on his scheduled photography trip in the city. When the DSP made contact and engaged him about preparation for the trip, Sergey reluctantly cooperated. With the TV episode still in his mind he struggled to say no to his favorite opportunity of the trip.

Since the DSP knew Sergey's routine very much he inquired from Sergey why he was reluctant to get his camera, vest, and extra battery in preparation of the trip. Sergey mentioned the TV episode regarding the paparazzi he had seen on TV. DSP assured Sergey that they were not going to take anyone's picture; that their focus was only on nature and beautiful landscapes not on people. Following some clarity and discussion, Sergey agreed to go with the DSP.

However, at their first scene, Sergey did not cooperate in taking any picture and after couple of minutes at their second scene Sergey insisted that he wanted to return to program. DSP tried but failed to have Sergey to photograph or to participate through *staged arrangement* which was different from all previous response from Sergey. Sergey, Boris, and the DSP returned to the program.

Sergey's response was a negative discovery when compared to his last response to the same staff action under the same circumstance where he did very well.

Generally, unexpected reactions can be that the overall situations of the individual have been altered by exposure to unpleasant experiences, personal preferences or medical matters from the period the service and support methods were adapted to the point the negative discovery is being observed.

b.   Negative discovery also results when the direct support process is characterized by the absence of effective staff action necessary to effect action needed toward meeting the individual's goal.

Consider the following scenario to help understand how ineffective staff action can contribute to negative discovery:

Scenario 3.12   *Negative discovery—Ineffective Staff Action*
Hillary is pursuing a communication goal and is currently working on first attaining a sign language skill to greet. DSP fails to include the NAMO features in the staff action, and is literally setting up a classroom style teaching approach with Hillary. DSP sits across the table from Hillary and begin to show and demonstrate various signs related to the skill of greeting.   Hillary continues to perform poorly from time to time and at present it seems as though Hillary has reach a point of stagnation as she is not in any way improving in any terms toward the skill of signing greetings. Although the DSP has the right materials and possess sign language knowledge, the approach to delivering the staff action is faulty.

Instead of creating the circumstance, stimulation, and facilitation across various settings, the DSP is only sitting at the table with Hillary trying to engagement her into all of the beautiful table activities even though the skill to sign greeting should not be limited to table activities.

Takeaway—23

To improve from a negative to positive discovery, DSP must first ensure that:

1. The goal is within the capacity of the individual
2. The appropriate contact and engagement techniques are applied with the individual
3. The staff action must include features of NAMO and that NAMO is applied accordingly.

---

iii. Determining Direct Discovery

Now that you are familiar with the categories of direct discoveries and the characteristics of response that each category covers, how do you determine what response is positive or negative?

a. Direct discovery is ascertained by comparing the individual's *last response* to the *current response* to the *staff action* at *the same level of support* under *similar circumstances*.

i. The current response is the individual's response on the present day

ii. The last response is the individual's most recent response since the last day the staff action was provided. The last response can be from a day or days before the present depending on when the individual was last supported toward the goal.

Consider the following scenario to help ascertain the category of direct discovery:

Scenario 3.13   *Categorizing discovery as Positive or Negative*

Agnes is working on a social skill to enable her to navigate simple conversation with her peers without bursting into tears. Agnes initiates and holds conversations with friends but often ends up crying when there is a disagreement about her subject of discussion.

On Monday, DSP had conversation with Agnes, role-played, and provided the needed reminders to Agnes. Later, DSP observed Agnes in conversation with her friends, however, Agnes ended up walking away from the discussion annoyed and almost crying. Immediately, DSP walked up to Agnes and initiated the appropriate conversation as part the staff action relevant to the goal.

On Tuesday and Wednesday, Agnes and her DSP went through their routine again and DSP created the appropriate opportunity initiating the circumstance for Agnes to interact and converse with her friends again. During both days, Agnes did very well, held conversations for longer than usual and then ended it cordially.

Following an absence on Thursday, Agnes attended program on Friday. DSP welcomed Agnes, made connection with her by asking about her absence and started engagement. DSP rendered staff action as required but Agnes refused to have any sort of interaction with anyone and even at one point did not want to continue the engagement with the DSP.

As seen from the above scenario, in the past week, Agnes cooperated and provided varied responses as anticipated by the staff action.

To determine whether there is any discovery, Agnes' current response to the staff action must be compared to her last response that was made under the same circumstance and support as the current response.

Diagram #19: Comparing Last and Current response

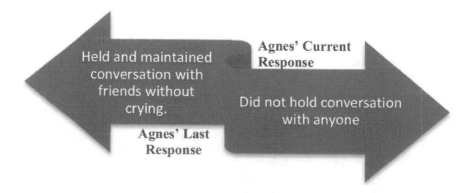

Held and maintained conversation with friends without crying.

Agnes' Last Response

Agnes' Current Response

Did not hold conversation with anyone

From the above diagram, Agnes' current response will be marked as a negative discovery in comparison to her last response in which she held and maintained conversation with friends without crying.

Takeaway—24

An event is not a discovery if it is not measure against some other similar events. When two or more events are measured against each other, the event with the more unique characteristics and feature is the discovered event.

Discovery must be used for team consumption by communicating with relevant players so as to draw everyone toward a system of continuity across the different settings and help maintain a sense of stability within the individual.

Scenario 3.13 is also shown on the following Discovery Worksheet depicting how the category of positive or negative is entered for program and compliance purpose.

3.   Discovery Worksheet

The discovery worksheet is a tool for quantifying responses and tabulating the categories of discoveries on a regular basis. The worksheet presents actual responses of from the individual through a given period of time.

The worksheet enables DSP to make reference to specific responses and aide in recalling the circumstance that surrounded the particular response. The discovery worksheet provides an excellent tool for comparing previous and current response. The worksheet qualifies the response while the categories of direct discovery quantifies it.

Discovery Worksheet

	Service/support (specific Staff Action provided toward the individual goal)	Response / Reaction To mark a response as *positive* or *negative discovery*, the Current response must be compare to the Last response.		Discovery	
		Last Response	Current Response	Positive	Negative
Monday	VO#1: Prompts, role-play to help in navigating simple conversation	Held and maintained conversation without ending up crying	Did not hold conversation with anyone	☐	☒
	VO#2: Prompts to clean self after meal	Threw emptied plate onto the floor	Refused to clean after self.	☐	☒
	VO#3: Prompts to shake hand instead of hugging	Shook hands instead of hugging	Shook hands instead of hugging	☒	☐
Tuesday	VO#1:			☐	☐
	VO#2:			☐	☐
	VO#3:			☐	☐
Wednesday	VO#1:			☐	☐
	VO#2:			☐	☐
	VO#3:			☐	☐
Thursday	VO#1:			☐	☐
	VO#2:			☐	☐
	VO#3:			☐	☐
Friday	VO#1:			☐	☐
	VO#2:			☐	☐
	VO#3:			☐	☐

Summary of Weekly Response: _____

Progress ☐
No Progress ☐

Staff name/signature: #1 _____ #2 _____ #3 _____

#4 _____

Daily Discovery Sheet   Week of _____ 2014

C

Summary of Chapter

1. DSP must constantly observe for outcomes of and reaction to support being provided during direct engagement with the individual. The ongoing process of discovery is a form of nonclinical assessment that informs and widens the supports mechanism for the individual; and suggests data that are relevant to maintaining or modifying current care plan.

2. When passive response becomes a routine it causes stagnation in the individual prospects and willingness to personally attempt initiating the task.

3. Partial participation does not required any role on the part of the individual other than being present. In a staged participation, the individual is actually performing actively toward the completion of the task. Participation under staged structure is important from each individual to ensure that the task reaches its stated goal.

4. Emotional, medical, and structural changes are the most common factors that contribute to a mute reaction.

5. Change in staff, tempered interaction from home or changes affecting relationship with peers or significant others can impact the emotions and affect the manner in which the individual react to direct support.

6. Changes in the structure of the operation of things may be unsettling from the onset of such change and are more likely to disrupt the flow of the individual's routine and subsequent reaction to staff engagement.

7. To improve from a negative to positive discovery, DSP must first ensure that:

    1. The goal is within the capacity of the individual

2. The appropriate contact and engagement techniques are applied with the individual (*See page 10 and Table #1 on page 12*)

3. The appropriate staff action includes features of NAMO and that NAMO is applied accordingly.

8. An event is not a discovery if it is not measure against some other similar events. When two or more events are measured against each other, the event with the more unique characteristics and feature is the discovered event.

4

chapter

Capability Vs Preference

OBJECTIVE OF THIS CHAPTER

By the end of this chapter, you will be able to demonstrate:

1. Understanding of the relationship and disparities between capacity and preference
2. Understanding of the different types of expectations and roles that expectations play in shaping preferences
3. Skills at harnessing the overlapping relationship between expectations, capability, and preferences to derive a desired outcome
4. Skills utilizing the skill-building approach and other tools to formulate effective plans
5. Understanding of the types of preferences
6. Knowledge of how to garner individual attention to a given task

A

Capacity vs Preference

Capacity and preference are two phenomena in an interdependent relationship. It is a relationship that is meant to support each component to make a whole. The relationship can be best viewed as an inseparable bond in which neither can progress without the other.

The progress in either capability or preference must be matched by a proportionate improvement in the other. The role of direct support from family, advocate or guardian and professional alike is irreplaceable in this process especially in creating the opportunity for actualizing the possibilities in balancing preference with capability and vice versa.

Creating the appropriate opportunity for balancing preference with capability can be overwhelming both for those providing the supports as well as the person for whom the support is intended especially when hopes and aspirations are set far from the realities of the person.

Unrealistic targets are usually unsustainable and they often put the individual's capacity and preference at odds and frustrates direct support efforts. Opportunities are endless, but like a race track, they have a starting line to begin with.

- ✓ When the creation of opportunities themselves are not coordinated with the prerequisites (i.e. capacity and preference) needed to carry them out, the often easy process of helping becomes a daunting one.

Diagram #20: Preference & Capability Relationship

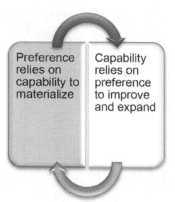

Preference relies on capability to materialize

Capability relies on preference to improve and expand

To understand the wedlock of capability and preference, we will need to delve into the controlling actors of hopes (i.e. expectations) and outcomes (i.e. results) impacting the quality of the capacity-preference paradigm.

Takeaway—25

The development of the individual must center on his ability and on his preferences (not on what is expected of him except he is being paid for meeting the expectations such as in an employment or under some other arrangement). The things that the individual can naturally do with little help are an asset to start with in the direct support process. Exposure also helps with discovering some of those things.

The more frequent and relevant the exposures, the more the areas of preferences increase.

Also, when exposure is based around the ability of the individual, subsequent preference formed will be less challenging to accomplish.

1. Expectations

Expectations and results are two actors that influence the quality of capability and preference. Expectation is what we hope to accomplish while a result is the actual outcome that is accomplished from our actions. An expectation is the driving force behind planned staff actions intended to yield a proportionate result.

Expectation is our hopes and aspirations of things we wish we possess or accomplish in a certain fashion we would appreciate more; it is usually not a goal but rather a probability of all of those things and possibilities for which there is a vision for fulfilment. This open-ended characteristic of expectation poses a challenge in setting a viable prospect of fulfilment.

Consider the *expectation for employment* in the diagram below.

Diagram #21: Employment Expectation

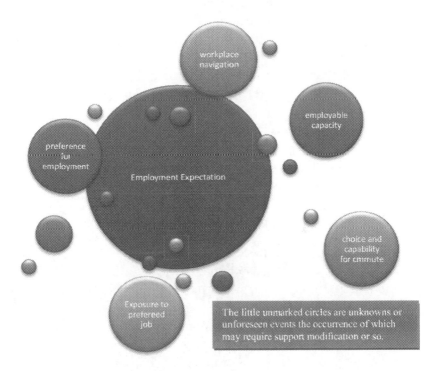

Expectation usually arises out of the ambition for accomplishing all of those desires that would make a given situation better than its current state.

But the desires themselves are not independent of the overall process involve in bettering the current situation. Therefore, the realization of the desire must be predicated upon the unique qualities of the individual which are mainly the individual's preference and capability.

Most of us set expectations for ourselves almost every time in our daily lives. Some expectations are short term while others are long term. Often we tend to set the expectations based either on our ability and willingness to follow through with our expectations, or we project our abilities upon the occurrence of some other events (i.e. opportunity) based upon which meeting the expectations will be possible.

However, despite the undeniable fact that people with intellectual and developmental disabilities are challenged with most of the everyday expectations we make, they also have about the same amount of demanding expectations like everyone else irrespective of their disabilities. There are personal expectations, expectations from friends and family members, and of course expectations from a range of service providers including day habilitation, residential, community habilitation, and other direct support service providers. For ourselves, we take caution in setting up so much high expectations for fear that failure to meet them could have moral and psychological consequences. However, we often overlook extending such consideration to the people we serve. Most of them are treated with such inconsideration so much that they are required to absorb similar amounts or more activities than those with whom they have no similar conditions.

i.   Personal expectations

Like everybody else, individuals with intellectual and developmental challenges do have expectations of their own only that there are some expectations that are more elaborate than others. Often for nonverbal individuals and those whose mode of communications are challenging to understand, there is no absolute certainty regarding their expectations at any given time, henceforth, some of the expectations are acted upon instead of hoping for it. This is even more challenging when the specific features of intellectual challenges are overwhelmingly overriding the ability of the individual.

Consider the following scenario to understand Personal Expectations:

> **Scenario 4.1   *Personal Expectation***
>
> Stacy comes to the day program from Monday to Friday. She has to wake up from bed at 6AM in order to have breakfast and make it on the scheduled 7:40AM transportation bus to program, and is usually at day program around 9AM. Like anyone else commuting on a bus for 80 minutes, she expects to relax and be accorded the appropriate respect. Once she gets to program, she uses the restroom, and heads to the kitchen to where she expects to get coffee. Then she expects her routines or review of how her day would look like instead of being shoved into some other things that she has no appropriate information of. In addition, she expects to be safely returned to her home unharmed. And generally, she expects to use the resources of the program when she wants; and so on.

Diagram #22: Personal Expectation

The above scenario and Diagram # 22 is filled with expectations that Stacy has for herself some of which she verbally expresses or only acts on them as a way of expression. There are certainly more that she expects of herself but her unexpressed expectations are overridden by her specific disabilities so much that continuous target exposure through direct support cannot be understated.

Also in the scenario, you will notice that Stacy's expectations are oriented toward her location and involvement at the time; and her expectation changes from setting to setting although the central issue remains focused on respecting and expressing her autonomy.

ii.   Family expectation

There are also expectations from friends and family members who are part of the individual life and support network. Family expectation arises out of the deeper knowledge, understanding, and relationship with the individual. Their experience with the individual's past, and unique opportunity that the family has had in interacting with the individual often places most families in the position to vouch on what they expect the individual should at least be able to do.

The family's expectations are further propelled by the needs to see the best for the individual who in the general view deserve much better than in any given state. Some family members tend to remember things that the individual had done couple of years ago or in recent times and still expects the individual to even do more. Some frown or become frustrated at the challenges obstructing their expectations. Family expectation is usually stretched than those of the service providers.

Using the *Personal Expectation* scenario above, we added the family expectation below to show how the diagram of expectations for Stacy expands:

> ### Scenario 4.2   *Family Expectation*
>
> Stacy comes to the day program from Monday to Friday. In addition to the facts in Scenario 4.1, Stacy's sister wishes Stacy can be taught how to do laundry; for Stacy to be able to clean the bathroom at least once a while; ADL for herself; do home chores; have a relationship someday; and at least learn the phone number among other things.

Diagram #23: Family Expectation

With the family expectation added to the diagram, Stacy becomes quietly overwhelmed but unfortunately her expression of such could be viewed as her unwillingness, which in most cases results in more layers of expectations added to deal with the issues of unwillingness. This, overall, can be a vicious cycle.

iii. Service providers' expectation

Then there is the service provider's expectation which is usually an incorporation of the individual's personal expectations and that of the family. Additionally, the service provider's expectation also reflects trends in the field to include any new definitions of terms and requirement for service provision to comply with. Some service providers even express their expectations in manners that appear as a policy requirement of the individual.

Consider the following scenario that adds the provider's expectations of Stacey:

Scenario 4.3	*Service Provider's Expectation*

Stacy comes to the day program from Monday to Friday. In addition to the facts in Scenarios 4.1 and 4.2, Stacy has a goal at the day program where she is working on improving her communications skills and learning social boundaries. These goals were derived as per Stacy's desire to be able to express herself clearly, and to be able to act calmly around her peers and respecting other people's personal space.

Additionally, some DSPs have their own expectations of Stacy. For instance when Stacey comes to program, and try to get her cup of coffee, the DSP usually gives Stacy a half filled cup while Stacy watches the DSP take a full cup for herself even though there's no clinical conditions that limit Stacy's consumption of coffee to a half cup. And although Stacy does know how get her own cup of coffee DSP does not allow her for fear that Stacy could get a full cup instead of a half cup, and also in the name of safety. Hence, Stacy is also expected to abide by the DSP's wishes.

Diagram #24: Service Provider's Expectation:

From the *Service Provider's Expectation* diagram above you get a visual of some of the typical expectations that are held for individuals receiving direct habilitation services although sometimes experience varies given the diverse nature of the field. The expectations for Stacy are enormous and may likely expand when other service providers such as community habilitation and residential services are included.

The challenge with extensive expectations is exacerbated by the fact that each of the expectations has its own unique layers of steps that are required to complete them. Even for the more ordinary task of "waking up from bed, readying for breakfast, and awaiting the transportation bus" require some basic capability and willingness in order to generate the outcome of presence.

Whatever the expectation is, it has to be met only with the feasibility that Stacy's capability offers. Feasibility is certain when the overlapping relationship of expectation, and capability and preference is properly implemented.

Diagram # 25: Overlapping Relationship

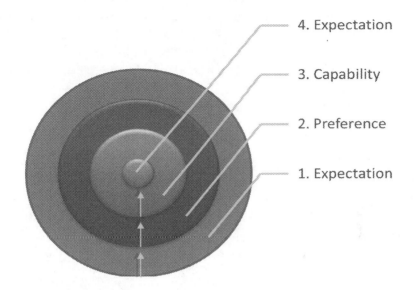

4. Expectation

3. Capability

2. Preference

1. Expectation

As shown in the diagram above, our relationship in the helping relationship starts with a broad expectations of both the overall relationship and of the specific purpose of the interaction.

In the diagram, the first layer is a broad open-ended expectation that tends to consume all of the honest efforts that is put into a direct support process. The Preference is next in size to the general expectations, followed by the capability. For individuals with intellectual and developmental disabilities, the capacity is usually the smallest in size as compare to the sizes of the expectation and the preference although capability remains the most critical component of empowerment.

However, when the expectation is narrowed down to fit within the size of the capacity, the expectation becomes realistically more likely to accomplish. The process of narrowing the expectation into a preference that fit within the capability so as to utilize the existing skills to implement the preference is known as the *The Now Factor (TNF)* method.

    iv. The Now Factor (TNF)

The Now Factor (TNF) is the method of streamlining the expectations to derive a preference through exposure to experiences that fits within the realm of the individual's existing capabilities. In direct support, a good portion of the support process includes contributing to setting up and working to meet expectations envisioned by a person or for a person who is challenged in doing so for himself or for one who cannot do it for himself at all. Like the expectations that we set for ourselves, the expectations we set for intellectually and developmentally challenged individuals require actions that must be based on their capability, not ours, to produce results—results whose full ramifications are unknown until it all sets in.

For most people receiving day habilitation services, the challenge lies in effectively sizing up the expectations into preference through exposure to cope with the capability to achieve the desired outcome. The Now Factor, in short is a skill formulated based on the existing capacity of the individual.

Consider the following scenario and help determine TNF skill.

Scenario 4.4   *TNF Skills*

Ben is an individual receiving day habilitation service. Ben has unsteady gait and uses a gait belt so that DSP can provide him physical support when ambulating. Ben has a condition that makes him to drool profusely; he is verbal but speaks the maximum of two words at a time and can say "bathroom" or "lunch" as well as simple greetings.

Ben also receives residential services and his residence wishes that Ben can be able to conduct basic ADL with little support and for him to be able to express himself. At present, Ben is able to wipe his drool when prompted to do so, and can communicate using limited 1-2 words.

In a development meeting, the habilitation manager explained to Ben the hopes and vision that his residence wants for him; and listed some areas that he may like to work on. When Ben was asked about what he prefers he nodded as if in affirmation to both the residence's wishes and the list of areas that the day habilitation manager presented.

Given the degree of drooling and how it sometimes get in the way of Ben's interactions with his peers, it was reasonably judged from Ben's perspective to have preferred to work on keeping him alert and aware of his drooling and wiping it up with minimum prompts overtime.

Considering the information in Scenario 4.4, let's determine the appropriate TNF skill that would be effective in accomplishing Ben's implied preference of being able to wipe his drool:

Table # 3: Determining TNF Skill

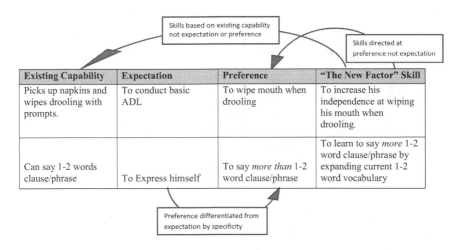

Existing Capability	Expectation	Preference	"The New Factor" Skill
Picks up napkins and wipes drooling with prompts.	To conduct basic ADL	To wipe mouth when drooling	To increase his independence at wiping his mouth when drooling.
Can say 1-2 words clause/phrase	To Express himself	To say *more than* 1-2 word clause/phrase	To learn to say *more* 1-2 word clause/phrase by expanding current 1-2 word vocabulary

In the table above, you will notice that the Residence's expectations are too broad and beyond Ben's existing capability. The expectations for Ben to conduct basic ADL and to express himself is very open-ended such that it will consume Ben's existing capability and willingness without producing any desired outcome. However, the expectations are narrowed in the Preference column by making it more specific which increases the chances of accomplishment.

Takeaway—26

Expectations play essential role in expanding an individual existing sets of preference by emphasizing the needs for more and more exposures to experiences intended to help the individual in forming more specific preferences.

However, a skill must not be built around the expectations because of its broad open-ended nature and its tendencies to overwhelm the capability.

Expectations always sound appealing and often signal how much we want of the individual. But it is important to remember that growing the skill must occur from inside out meaning that expanding the skill should start within the current set of skills and extends outward.

In the following diagram, you will see the illustration of how to grow or expand the skill from inside out. From Ben's current skills, the TNF method can be used to acquire new skills by building upon the existing ones.

Diagram #26: TNF skills building method

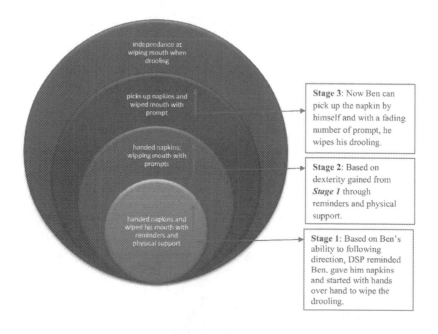

In Table #3, the expectation of ADL involves series of activities that must be broken down into manageable pieces to make it easier to achieve. Expectation must be narrowed down to be result-oriented. It is a circular process wherein in order for the expectation to be results-oriented, the expectations will have to be condensed into a specific preference.

Takeaway—27

If an expectation is condensed into a preference but the resulting preference is not within the capacity of the individual, DSP must shift the focus of the experiences that the individual has been exposed as a result of the preference. DSP must ensure that the experience affords the individual some types of role other than mere exposure to partial participation.

2. Result and consequence

Result is the eventuality that occurs as the particular ramification of a staff action. The specificity of a result must be particularly certain. When a result produces the target goal it is likely to have the consequences intended but if the result does not produce the target goal it will produce unintended consequences.

Consider the following scenario to help understand result and goal:

Scenario 4.5   *Result and consequence*

Joe is a verbal individual who is fairly independent at accomplishing activities of daily living on his own. Based on Joe's level of functioning and his love for music, Joe became part of local music group at the Ginger Bread Community Center with the goal of further enhancing his skills and knowledge in the use of the tambourine his favorite musical instrument. Staff actions were formulated to ensure Joe is adequately supported. After few weeks, Joe had found renewed interest in the music group. Although the music group runs 11Am to 2PM, Joe wants to be there from the moment he gets off the transportation bus.

> Every effort to help Joe understand the timeframe and the idea of beginning and end or start and finish have not been successful. Now if he is not taken to the music group he would be disruptive and would refuse to engage in anything else including the activities he had been exposed to earlier. Even for the goal of exposure to learn new skills with relevant musical instruments is not yielding any progress.

From the above scenario you can see that the result from the action intended to help Joe did not meet the target goal of the exposure, and as a result, unintended consequences are being experienced.

Diagram #27- Result

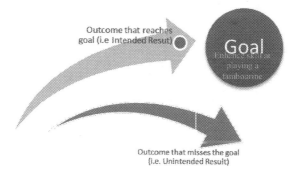

Result is not necessarily the same as a goal as seen depicted in Diagram #27. A goal is fixed and any outcome short of the specific content of the goal is not a goal. Although a goal can be modified, the consequence of the modification is fixed and is itself a goal until it is further visited. A result that reflects the content of the target goal becomes a goal and a result that does not reflect the exact content of the goal is an unintended result.

Diagram #28- Tasks segments

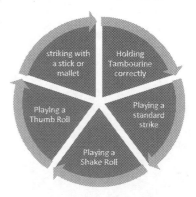

And even when the goal is divided into segments as shown in Diagram #28, each segment is a goal all by itself such that when a result does not meet the requirement of the current segment, the consequence is said to be unintended.

Also in Diagram #28, you will notice that the goal of enhancing the skills at playing the tambourine requires at least five tasks. The completion of each task is by itself a goal that must be met.

The occurrence of an unintended result of a staff action can start showing up sometimes immediately after the inception of the staff action and other times at the conclusion of the staff action. On the other hand if the intended result of a staff action begin to show before the conclusion of the staff action, the entire process will be considered effective. Sometimes the results are unintended, and other times it is underachieved or not achieved at all.

The unintended result of Joe's exposure (in Scenario 4.5) could have been curtailed if Joe was introduced to the music group before the transition. The introduction would have informed the setting up of the appropriate staff support. From the facts in the scenario, Joe undertook the participation without full appreciation of the expectations of not only the music group but also the day program. Before Joe was made to start with the music group, DSP should have ensured that Joe was introduced to the opportunity before transitioning him to it:

1) Introduction before transition:

    Introducing Joe to the music group should have been preceded by familiarizing him with opportunity leads such as paying visit to the event; holding conversation about whether Joe would like the event even if DSP has reason to believe that the Joe likes it. During the introduction, DSP continuously observe for verbal or nonverbal clues and expression unique about Joe's reaction. DSP must be particular in observing as to ascertain Joe's level of interest, for example, in asking about the opportunity, offering to stay longer than planned or to stay indefinitely; making inquiry about returning to the opportunity. For nonverbal individuals, DSP should observe for nonverbal expression of interest unique to the individual. Some general nonverbal expression of interest includes:

    a) The act of touching or feeling things at the location of the opportunity;
    b) interaction of others relevant to location;
    c) attentive viewing;

d) attempts at reaching for things when reaching is not a behavioral concern;
e) exhibiting the sense of excitement;
f) refusal to leave or insistence on staying;
g) relating to the content or people at location;
h) exhibiting less anxiousness; and demonstration of calmness

The individual's reaction helps to inform the appropriate staff action relevant to supporting the individual toward the particular opportunity.

2. Demarcation and differentiation:

Additional visits to the opportunity so as to create the sense of demarcation and differentiation of locations. The additional visits can be centered on enhancing Joe's understanding the purpose of the opportunity as well as the expectations governing participation such as the simple rules. DSP must ensure that these things are explained to Joe while at the scene in a manner that is respectful, specific, and personalized.

3. Action and consequence:

DSP can also discuss consequences with Joe and make effort to create scenarios that are more likely to occur at the scene. One way of doing so can involve arranging to be turned back (not being allowed in) at a certain time and to be dismissed at a given time. For instance, if the group starts at 10AM, and DSP and Joe get there 30 minutes late by 10:30AM, they should be made to return and provided explanation for why they cannot sit with the group. The DSP will already be aware of this since it is the DSP that made the arrangement as a way of teaching consequence. This is necessary especially if Joe does not have an abstract understanding of consequence. DSP must explain to the individual each time an action producing consequence occurs.

Most results will have unintended consequences. However, the impact of the unintended consequences can be well planned for or contained from the very initiation of the action.

Exposure to new participation must include accounting for all of the known possible contingencies that are likely to occur if the target participation is either overly performed or under appreciated.

Results are based on the actions that fuel them. An action that is appropriately planned with a realistic expectation in mind produces the results appropriate to the action.

The complete ramifications of an individual's involvement must be considered especially when the individual's participation is the first at the particular opportunity.

We tend to ignore or pretend as though failure doesn't exist sometimes out of the wishful thinking that thinking anything other than positive will impede the positive from occurring.

B

___

Preference

A preference is simply an individual's choice based on past experiences or on encounters with new and ongoing exposures. Exposure creates awareness which in turn makes expressing or understanding a preference possible. Usually, the purpose of exposure is to build the individual's areas of preferences for which the individual's existing capability can be used to enhance the individual's overall autonomy and community belongingness.

Typically, an individual encounter more experiences to form preferences as compared to improvement in the capacity. Although preference diminishes overtime as capacity fades, a lot of artifacts of the individual's past, present, and developing life events play transformative role in the choices made as well as what sentiment that the individual expresses toward a given matter. A preference, therefore, always overweighs capability. This disparity is in of itself the best opportunity for the application of capability.

Consider the following scenario to help understand how the disparity between preference and capability is important in basing service goal on those preferences that are within the capability of the individual:

Scenario 4.5   *Disparity: Capability vs Preference*
Marc is an independent gentleman in terms of completing nearly all of his activities of daily living by himself. Nearly all of the DSP wants to work with Marc. He is helpful in terms of encouraging his peers to take part in activities as a form of peer-support, and he requires no physical support at all.

However, Marc is challenged in understanding personal boundaries. Although he does not mean harm when he touches others, he would tap or hold anyone by the hand and say "hi" and will start laughing hysterically. Additionally, Marc is limited in terms of communicating full sentences of his choice of things. He talks very fast and for most people, he repeats himself three or more times before he can be understood except you are used to Marc and are familiar with his pronunciations and speech patterns. Additionally, Marc does not know how to stop once he embarks on something and sometimes requires physical intervention such like getting between him and the task and telling him to end it.

Marc wants to be a cashier. And he also wants to work in the Post Office to sort out mail as well as have an intimate relationship (a girlfriend). Marc also wants to be able to travel by himself not only to the program but also around the program community by himself without any DSP because he says DSP always gets in his way and tells him to stop when he tries to talk to a girl on the street.

According to the above scenario, Marc has the following capabilities: ADL skills, communicates, and he prefers the following: cashier, post man; a girlfriend; and traveling independently.

Diagram #: 29: Capacity-Preference Disparity

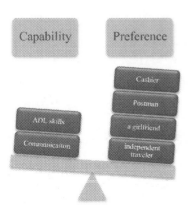

From the disparity diagram you will notice that weighing the preference against the areas of capability helps more in seeing that the capability of communication is key to nearly all of Marc's current set of preferences.

The capacity-preference disparity gives the capacity a lot more room to be applied to any or all of the options that numerous preferences offer.

1. Types of preferences

There are two types of preference: expressed preference and implied preference.

a. Expressed Preference (EP)

A preference that is communicated by the individual receiving services is an expressed preference. The method of such communication varies from individual to individual based on unique cognitive and communicative abilities. Depending on the individual, the preference can be communicated nonverbally through signs and clear gestures as nodding; through speech, or by writing. A perfect example is Scenario 3.1 in chapter 3 where Amy is expressing her dreams of being a waitress. EP is straightforward and the individual is the master of her services when she has clearly expressed what she wants. The service provider listens and follows the dreams and aspiration of the individual as realistically as possible.

Sometimes difficulty arises out of the process of providing services directed at meeting the dreams and the individual's predisposition when the individual's expression is not realistic at the moment the preference is expressed. For instance, a legally blind individual in the day program has expressed the preference of learning to cook as well as operate her television at home; then there is another who wants to be a police officer. When an individual is not exposed to as many events and things to help with expanding the horizons of making choices, numerous preferences are expressed out of utilizing what the individual already has available to him/her.

i. Opportunity Leads and Preference

Ordinarily DSPs do not merely pick up an individual and go around showing them to new experiences. A good practice is to create some sort of awareness within the individual as it relates to what is going on or what is about to go on and to ascertain whether there will be an expression of interest from the individual. This is necessary not only to prepare the individual for the opportunity but to also show respect to the individual's person. Sometimes, an individual smiles or frowns, nods in agreement or disagreement, or directly verbalizes approval or disapproval to the prospective events when DSP affords the opportunity to do so. During this process, whatever is said or done to stimulate the individual into responding to the suggestion for the opportunity is called an opportunity lead. Opportunity Leads (OL) are baits of clues and hints to new experiences through the introduction of the exposures. The purpose of an OL is to help the individual express a preference or interest in an activity. OL is generally any action that encourages an individual into taking part in an exposure. Some examples of opportunity leads are travel training assessments, assessment for augmentative communication or adaptive devices as well as ordinary conversation with the individual about an activity before the activity takes place.

Opportunity leads can be:

✓ Conversations about the exposure.

Introduction to the exposure can be made through any means of communication uniquely appreciated by the individual so as to conjure the individual's attention and interest in a way that is not aversive.

✓ Videos or photographs of the exposure

How does the exposure look like? How will involvement in it feels? How exciting will the experience be? For instance, Ginger Bread community center is a potential volunteer site that the individual would benefit from. Wouldn't it be the right thing to do to let the individual get some exciting information about Ginger Bread community center in addition to the talks about destination and the purpose of the travel? It is good practice to provide as much information as possible to the individual. Pictures of the destination or video presentation of tasks that are carried out at the scene are prefect OL.

✓ Contacts (either soft or hard contact): Make contact with the goal of invoking the individual's attention to the purpose of the contact.

Sometimes exposure is not about a destination. Exposure can also be about introduction to new activities such as those happening around the individual or those that are needed and relevant to a new goal. For instance, some individuals will gravitate towards a piano keyboard than the virtual piano keyboard on iPad, others might do the opposite. But putting the two side by side will attract the individual's attention into making a selection.

Refer to Scenario 1.2 & 1.3 in Chapter 1 for examples of soft and hard contacts.

✓ Spontaneous experience

Spontaneity holds well for some individuals. Irrespective of the conversation and the number of relevant information provided about the exposure, some individuals reacts even more positively to being physically a part and experiencing the exposure than they would when the exposure is introduced to them. Trips and community exploration is an example of spontaneous experience.

Spontaneous experience also includes natural, unstructured or unplanned activities presented to the individual out of the assumption or insinuation that the individual will prefer it to any current activities in the works.

b.   Opportunity Lead and technology software

Sometimes the OL themselves can be exposures. This usually occurs when the opportunity lead involves the performance of the exposure. Assistive technology software are perfect example. Technological software and hardware are usually opportunity leads that involve the participation and performance by the individual. Even though the assistive technology is a lead to which the individual is being exposed, the introduction of the tool goes beyond explanation or video presentation to include the actual tryout in order to determine the individual's reaction or the appropriateness of the technology to the individual.

Consider the following scenario to help understand relationship between of opportunity lead and technology:

Scenario 4.6	*Opportunity Lead and technology*

Shanna enjoys listening to merengue, bachata, and oldies Spanish music, using iPad, computer, and dancing. She is verbal; and she does light maintenance volunteering task at the Ginger Bread day care program. Shanna is working on learning to maintain social boundaries, making healthy choice, as well as using the telephone to learn to dial 911 as well as the number to her residence.

> DSP presents Shanna with an iPad as an opportunity lead in order to help her work with her goals. For the goals that Shanna is working on, the DSP used a tool to help collect the requisite information to help with finding the appropriate applications that Shanna can use as part of working on her goals. The DSP identified applications such as Everyday Social Skills; Learn My Info *(Phone #); and* ABC Food. The three applications are directly related to Shanna's day habilitation goals.
>
> Here, the three applications are now Shanna's goal instead of just being an opportunity lead. She may choose to use or not use them in which case DSP will explore other alternatives, but once she uses them, her use of the application has gone beyond mere introduction to actual use. Hence her use of the technology will constitute her working on her goals.

Nowadays, most curricula and goal related activities are being computerized and made accessible on iPads, computers and other PDAs. Also there are assistive technology equipment such as plate guard, adaptive spoons and pens, to augmentative communication devices that are all opportunity leads that rely on practical use on the part of the individual. Often adaptive and augmentative equipment are clinically sanctioned. With the exception of clinically approved devices which are made available following some forms of assessment, opportunity leads to all other forms of assistive technology are themselves exposures. Assessment is a form of opportunity lead when it is conducted to determine the appropriate fit of the device for an individual or to ascertain the individual's level and understanding of the device.

Acquiring the right technology and software that match an individual's existing capability and preference is one of the purposes of opportunity leads. The common mistake that is often committed is that the DSP's attempt at trying to match the individual to a given technology instead of matching the technology to what the individual currently possess in terms of capability and interests. Without the need for clinical procedures and requirements, most DSPs regularly utilize everyday technology such as the iPad, personal computers, mac, as well as certain handheld personal information managers (PIM) to support individuals.

Often with these everyday technology that requires no clinical clearance for their usage, locating the appropriate software to be used as part of the direct support effort is most challenging. DSPs are caught up with time in their effort to research, identify and then tryout applications with individuals only to find out that the application is not only inappropriate but could cause unintended consequences regarding the individual's interest in using the technology.

The grid as shown below is a worksheet with dual purposes. It is a tool for determining the appropriate software or applications that not only match the individual's existing capacity but also contained the possibility to stimulate enhancement since the applications will be based on the individual's goal. The grid can also be used as a communication tool for DSP so as to maintain the desired level of congruity and continuity in the support process. Most of the information needed for completion of the grid is already available elsewhere in the individual's service folder. What the grid does is to summon information about the individual's goal, interests, and capability into a single form. The Grid below is a sample of what information to collect using the goal:

Table # 6: The Grid

The Grid
Matching technology to individual

Ginger Bread Community Daycare Center
Staff Caseload

Updated 4/30/2014

Staff: Perez Perry

Individual Names	Interest/Favorite/preference	Capabilities & Communication	Individualized Goals	Current Community involvement	Previous Use of Assistive Tech & Purpose	Recommended Computer/Ipad Applications
Marnie Z	Likes to do arts/crafts	Can go out on short trips	1. Personal care 2. Community safety 3. Healthy choice making	Likes going out in community	Drawing	1. Let's Learn How To Draw 2. Community Signs & Words 3. ABC Foods
Moses M	Short trips; singing; drawing; parties; dancing	Verbal; occasional signing;	1. Improve artistic ability 2. Improve communication 3. To make friends	Enjoys CIO, volunteer, short community trips	Community signs; musical instrument; drawing	1. Let's Learn How to Draw 2. Auryn Ink 3. Conversationbuilder 4. ASL Coach
Shanna V	Listening to oldies Spanish music, using Ipad, computer, dancing	Verbal, volunteering; light maintenance	1. social boundary 2. Healthy choice making 3. Using telephone	Enjoys CIOs but needs supervision due to visual defects	Listens to merengue; bachata	1. Everyday Social Skills 2. My Daily Tasks 3. Learn My Info (Phone #) 4. ABC Food 5. QuickCues
Roy O	Talking about his old time favorite shows; likes own space	Verbal; short community trips	1. Community safety 2. Improve ADL skills 3. Better communication	Community exploration	None	1. Sign 4 Me 2. Model Me Going Places 3. Practicing Street Crossing

What Do the Above Individuals Share Together as a Group?

Common Activities In This Group
1. Dance Exercise
2. Conversation about purchasing favorites
3. Conversation about TV news (especially CBS News)
4. Drawing/doodling/painting

Common Favorite Destinations of this Group
1. Movie Theatre
2. Ginger Bread Senior Center
3. Neighborhood Park

Volunteering/Community contribution by group or any of its members?
What: NONE   Where: _____

Favorite Group Activities
1. Conversation about food choices & post-community experience
2.
3.

iii. Opportunity Lead as a goal

OL can also be a standalone and be considered as a goal by itself. Since the purpose of OL is to stimulate the individual into some other activities for which there is an existing capacity to participate, individuals who exhibit severe cognitive and communicative impairment with demonstrative challenges to engage in any activity can be consistently expose to different experiences.

When an individual is consistently introduced to new opportunity leads so as to discover more about what the individual likes and capable of doing, the implication of the individual's exposure becomes a goal of the staff action.

Consider the following scenario to help understand how a goal can be about opportunity leads:

Scenario 4.7	*Opportunity Lead and goal*

Einstein functions in the range of severe intellectual disability. He exhibits very severe inability to focus even during meal. Due to his extreme lack of attention or ability to focus, he is both fed and assisted with changing regularly in the bathroom. However, Einstein is physically stable and requires no support in ambulating except that he needs to be held because due to his inability to focus he demonstrates complete unawareness of his surroundings. Further compounding the challenge of interaction with Einstein is his communicative limitation. Einstein is nonverbal and lacks any known mode of communication at this point. Also, although DSP has been working with Einstein for about year, DSP has not been successful in discovering anything from Einstein as far as engagement is concerned. Family members but especially mom and dad who are more involved with Einstein have all admitted to knowing anything other than that Einstein likes pacing and rocking around in the home. Einstein has not been said to be attracted to any of the activities that he has been exposed to thus far. His reactions to experiences are completely passive.

However, in the continued effort to observe and discover even the littlest things that attract Einstein, DSP consistently introduces opportunity leads to Einstein ranging from assistive technology, to conversation, to community inclusion opportunities. The concentration on exposure to different experiences directed at enabling better staff action to support Einstein is the goal that is being worked on. As a result Einstein's goal is stated as follows: "Einstein would like to explore available community and technological resources so as to receive more appropriate support."

Diagram # 30: Opportunity Lead as a goal

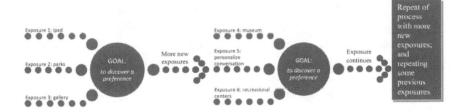

The things that stimulate one person may not necessarily stimulate another, and as such OL must be specific to each person especially when OL is used as a goal. As it is for most direct support efforts, the challenge to OL is the extreme limitation in the ability to focus. Some individuals can entertain very little attention to almost anything including the most essential activity of feeding. It is not that the individual possess no attention span but it is such that the available attention span is severely insufficient to generate any interests from the individual toward the OL. The situation becomes even more complicated when the inability to focus is compounded by other severe functional challenges.

As we will discuss later in this chapter, there is always some forms of activities that are appropriate for almost every level of capacity. Hence, instead of the challenge being the individual's inability to focus, the challenge is actually that the level of exposure or OL is beyond the individual's existing capability to focus.

In cases where an individual has insufficient attention span, DSP must apply spontaneous exposure. This means that the individual will be exposed to new experiences by practically trying to engage them in the midst of the process. Often short or no attention is a result of medical conditions not necessarily that the individual is doing so out of unwillingness to engage with the activity.

    b.   Implied Preference (IP)

Unlike expressed preference, an implied preference is not communicated in any ways by the individual due to severe inability to produce an expression; but it is rather inferred from either the individual's action, the unique circumstances surrounding the individual's current situation or from the individual's past history of similar preferences.

Implied preference cannot be based upon by the operational needs of any service provider and must not be influenced by policies or actions of the providers. A habilitation provider cannot adopt or influence the adoption of an implied preference for an individual only because such preference places the provider in complaint with its policy requirement.

Implied preference is one of the greyest areas in the direct support process. It is rarely referred to as being implied even though it is widely derived and implemented on behalf of those individuals that are plagued by severe cognitive and communicative deficiencies.

There is a golden rule known as SEAMAN that guides the adoption of an implied preference. The golden rule is that the preference must be the best of available alternatives such that the individual would have reasonably made similar preferences only if there was the ability of express it overtly.

The available alternatives must *reflect* SEAMAN:

1. *Safety*: Physical and psychological wellbeing of the individual.
2. *Empowering*: Past or current experiences from which individual gains positive enhancement and empowerment
3. *Ability*: The existing capability of the individual to perform.
4. *Medical Situation*: The most recent clinical and medical situation of the individual.
5. *Agreement*: Consensus of the family, guardian, and/or advocate.
6. *Needs Manifested*: Unnegotiable necessities of the individual across relevant settings.

The implied preference must be based on the most recent information available for each SEAMAN component.

Consider the following scenario to help understand implied preference:

Scenario 4.7 *Implied preference*

Wendy is senior citizen receiving services at the Ginger Bread Adult day care program. Wendy is nonverbal and does not understand sign language. Wendy understands a few action words when spoken to her such as come, let's go, '*bathroom*', eat, have a seat, and put on your coat. Other than responding to some of those action words, she does not respond to any other communication involving explanation of actions or to questions in any manner as she is not able to gesture like nodding. If Wendy is in disagreement of an "action word" she would not perform it. For instance if a DSP say to Wendy, please have a seat, Wendy would not sit if she does not agree with sitting in the particular space.

Wendy had recently underwent refractive surgery to improve her eye sight and it is recommended that she must be protected from condition that would might cause irritation to her eye such as windy and dusty environs. She does not walk more than two blocks regardless of weather conditions. Wendy feeds herself and does most ADL on her own. She enjoys striking the piano keyboard as there is a family piano at home which she has been exposed to. At home Wendy clears the table after meals, and sometimes she can get her own cereal in the morning. At the program, Wendy displays no behavior of concern and she is usually in agreement with almost every suggestion that DSP makes on her behalf as far engaging in activities and going community trips are concern.

DSP and family have not identified anything as something that Wendy dislikes. She is very agreeable. Wendy does make some grinding sounds but she does it so often and randomly that it is difficult to tie it to anything in her surrounding or to a reaction to a staff action. Wendy is physically stable and requires no physical support.

From the above fact, what preference would Wendy adopt for herself if she could express it? Now that the situation is such that Wendy cannot express what she would like to be supported on, what preference can be inferred from Wendy's action and support cycle?

Note that preference is the basis upon which the individual's service goal is set. Hence, to set Wendy's day habilitation goal, the golden rule of implied preference must be taken into account. DSP must apply the SEAMAN golden rule to Wendy's scenario in order to derive an implied preference.

The golden rule does not focus on challenges to help infer an implied preference. This is because the severity of the individual's disability is the chief reason why a preference is being inferred from the individual's action and surrounding situations. As you will also notice from the SEAMAN form below, the Safety and Medical /Clinical components are not reflected in the implied preference. This is because most individuals in the day habilitation setting are not concentrated on working on medical issues even though services are provided to as to preserve or improve on the individual's situation as is medically sanctioned. Consider the sample table below:

Table #7: SEAMAN Implied Preference Form

Name of Individual: Wendy J.

Date of form: 4/30/2014

Safety (Current concern for Physical and psychological wellbeing)	Empowerment (Past and current experiences from which enhancement and empowerment were gained)	Ability (Existing capabilities that would make performance possible)	Medical/Clinical (most recent clinical and medical situation of the individual)	Agreement/consensus (specify issues for which there is consensus of the family, guardian, and/or advocate)	Needs Manifested (unnegotiable daily necessities of the individual across relevant settings)
1. Ensuring Wendy is not taken advantage of due to her inability to communicate overtly 2. Cannot walk more than 2 city blocks at any given time.	1. Clearing meal table at home 2. Feeding herself	1. Ability to follow action words 2. Ability to not follow action words when in disagreement 3. Fairly independent ADL skills 4. Able to strike piano keyboard 5. Feeds herself once she is served 6. Clears meal table at home 7. Gets along with DSP and group members	1. Communicate with DSP 2. Learning sign language	Wendy's sister wants Wendy to improve on: 1. Serving herself with cold food like salad, cereal; 2. Clearing the table at least after herself 3. Learning to sign simple words relevant to her routine *Note:* Wendy's sister is only family left who is involve with servicer providers, and has been directly involved with Wendy for 10 years.	Refractive surgery – must be protected from windy and dusty environs to avoid irritation of the eye

Implied Preferences
It is implied that:
1. Given that Wendy performs action words but unable to express her disagreement, she would benefit from learning sign language for basic everyday words relevant to her routine.
2. Considering that Wendy is able to feed herself once she is served, she would benefit from learning to make cold lunches such as sandwich on her own.
3. Since Wendy currently cleans after herself after a meal, however, she spills stuff from the table to the floor because of which she would benefit from improving on that skill to clean properly after meals.

Exposure is accomplished in many forms depending on the individual. The most common forms of exposing individuals to new experience is through community trips, sightseeing, and any other forms of interactions with the community or a target experience. However, the nature of community exposure varies from person to person as most efforts are squarely focus on interaction with the community.

2. Community Inclusion vs Community Participation

There are continuous attempts to expose individuals to community opportunities often with the goal of creating new experiences for the individuals directed toward community integration. Understanding opportunities that individuals get exposed to will serve to devise more appropriate community opportunities that reflect a common goal for those whom the experience is meant. Part of that understanding is contingent upon knowing the two major components of community integration—inclusion and participation. Community integration is one of the core of the wholesale social movement of direct habilitation. Community inclusion and the community participation are two major components of community integration. However, the two are not the same although most DSPs treat community inclusion to mean the same as community participation.

Community inclusion is essentially an exposure to the unrestricted space that every community member has access to. Community inclusion means access to the public space provided for anyone to access. For instance, access to the park means that you are included in the right to be at the park. In short, community inclusion is accessing the community as you should in ways that do not exclude you. Community inclusion all by itself does less to foster integration as it is not the same as improving the sense of belongingness because it is less involving in terms of creating the feelings that community members have for each other. Community integration is not achieved with only one of the components. Often, individuals are sent into the wilderness of the community to access their unexclusiveness and to explore and connect with anything that stimulates them into appreciating the inclusive experience thereof.

However, community inclusion expands an individual's areas of preference and for many individuals it leads to community participation. One way to expand a person's areas of preferences is by exposing them to things that educate, excite or stimulate them, or motivating them into increasing existing involvement, renewing experience, or contributing to community.

Diagram #31: Community Integration

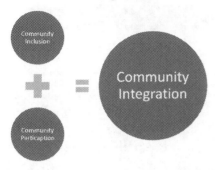

Community integration is meant to foster the sense of belonging within the individual. What this means is that DSP must create the circumstances that makes the individual to feel part of the community. Often, most DSP are centered on trying to make the individual fit in instead of belonging. One of the cores of integration is not to fit in with everyone else but rather to belong there. To fit in means that the individual will have to relearn almost every time he visits a new destination in order to fit in. Doing so is bound to overcome the essence of the experience because of the undue pressure that goes into trying to adjust to the requirement of fitting in.

Belonging is a human need and it is essentially about being a part of a community that as a whole is greater than the individual person. Inclusion and participation serve that need whether it is immediately noticed from the individual's reaction or not. DSP must also ensure that exposure minimizes the prospects of needing help from community members or exhibiting interactions that have the propensity to interfere with the need to belong. Unlike community inclusion which has general public expectations, community participation usually have strict location-specific expectations as to how participation is carried out and managed. As it is with most of direct support, inclusion and participation are part of an ongoing process that usually strengthen each other.

Consistent inclusion increases the prospect for participation for most individual. In most cases when an individual is directly involved with participation without preliminary exposure, unintended outcome is experience. As shown in Diagram #26, the goal of the participation will be less likely to achieve when participation is undertaken without introduction which inclusion provides.

Consider the following examples to better understand the difference between the two:

Table # 8: Inclusion vs Participation

Community Inclusion	Community Participation
An exploration of the local coffee shops in the neighborhood	Purchasing a cup of coffee from the local coffee shop
A trip to the parks	A picnic or some activities at the park
A trip to the mall	Making purchases or windowing shop at the mall
A trip to a performance or show	Performing at the show
A walk to the farmer's market	Selling or purchasing from the farmer's market
—	Volunteering of any kind is a participation
Going to the gallery	Having an art show or having one's arts in the gallery
Bowling alley	Playing bowling
Exposure to museum	Participation in the purpose of the location/to view artifacts/history
A trip to the cinema or restaurant	Participation in the purpose of the location/new experience and activities

C

Capacity

Now that you have covered preference and learn how to cultivate it, we will now discuss the other half of the relationship without which the preference is a nonmaterial. Capacity is the individual's ability and willingness based upon which a preference materializes. Simply put, pages fill with preference is nothing when there is no existing capacity to initiate working on it. Both capacity and preference cannot be developed at the same level for an individual with intellectual and developmental disabilities. It is either that there is an existing capacity and exposure is being undertaken so as to cultivate a preference in which the capacity can be applied and enhanced, or it has to be that there is already a preference and the individual is supported in order to develop the skill to make the preference possible.

A classic example is Scenario 2.13 where the individual Maria has the capacity to answer and transfer phone calls, and answer questions from visitors. Maria has the capacity needed to work or volunteer as a receptionist. Consider that what is lacking is that Maria's ability is not accompanied by the willingness or preference to work or volunteer as a receptionist at a local senior center. Then consider the reverse of the situation in which Maria has the preference to work as a receptionist but lacks the capacity needed to undertake and complete the minimum task with minimum support.

A development in capacity (such as the ability to answer and transfer phone calls, and answer questions from visitor in the example above) can be appropriately explored so as to create the proportionate enhancement within the preference. Let's refer to the Scenario 2.13 again and this time let's consider that Maria can be exposed to any available opportunities so as develop her preference in which she can utilize her skills more beneficially. This is discussed in Diagram #11 in detail.

It should be noted that it is less challenging to create the proportionate enhancement within the individual's preference to match the evolving capacity than it is with the reverse. This is because a preference is increasingly flexible as it is a factor of the individual's level of exposure to their surrounding and options of support curricula.

Takeaway—28

DSP must properly record the preferences of the individual so as to maintain a resource manual that can be used as a reference because the more information there is about what the individual likes the richer the direct support process will be.

Capacity is less flexible because it is the function of the individual's overall condition. Although capacity is define here as a person's ability and willingness to perform a preference, the phenomena is more than that considering it from the unique perspective of each individual with intellectual disabilities. Nonetheless, there is always some forms of capacity that every person possesses only that the challenge lies in discovering it. To discover a fuller capacity, the individual's current skill set must be gradually expanded upon through consistent exposures to new experiences that reflect current and emerging needs.

Capacity is so essential in the capacity-preference paradigm that sometimes no amount of preference can be developed without the capacity to do so. The individual's current skillset is considered as the requisite skill.

Consider the preference of making necklaces which involves at least the task of passing a beading wire through a couple of beads; or the ability to make a patterned necklace out of blue and white beads.

What existing capacity or does that the individual needs to possess in order to accomplish the preference?

The minimum or requisite existing capacity/skill set that the individual needs to have include: Capacity of sight; adequate level of attention/ Fine motor skills.

Based on the existing capacity/skill set, DSP can focus on establishing effective engagement and providing staff action on identifying, setting up the materials, and making the patterned beads.

➤ Capacity can be enhanced through the dexterity of a given skill or through exposure to unique learning opportunity relevant to the skills required to realizing a preference.

Dexterity requires handiness on the part of the DSP and performance ability on the individual's part.

✓ An individual can always have dexterity with a given task or series of tasks when the conduct of the task is structured based upon a relevant existing skill set that the individual possesses.

For instance, consider an individual with the preference for making necklace, and also consider that the individual possessed the minimum or requisite existing capacity required for the task involved in making a necklace such as passing a beading wire through a couple of beads. Dexterity results when the individual repeatedly accomplish the task over and over again.

However, sometimes most capacities are so deeply hidden such that its discovery is dependent upon unveiling a host of other personally unique characteristics of the individual.

Refer to the necklace example again and consider that while DSP has been supporting the individual, a range of other unique characteristics such as vocalizing the names of the items involved in the task or the tendency to take control of the task or some other things, has been uncovered. Hence, while working to support the individual into the necklace activity those other things were uncovered as well.

➤ Every stage of development within the individual is embedded with a unique set of capabilities that impact the individual's control of his activities of daily living.

Hence, the individual's development in being able to accomplish the necklace task is a result of the requisite skills that the individual initially had before starting the task.

i. Meaningfulness Vs appropriateness

Meaningfulness must not be confused with appropriateness

> Meaningfulness means that the experience is empowering or has features that would contribute to the enhancement of the individual or lead to a positive experience.

Example: volunteering

> Appropriateness refers to relevance in terms of *both* age and capability.

Example: volunteering (volunteering is age appropriate for all adult but the adult must also be capable to be appropriate for volunteering).

Discrepancy between the meaningfulness and appropriateness of an activity will lead to a negative experience. When the activity is unfitting or inappropriate for the individual, there will be no performance. Usually this is not because the individual lacks any capacity it is mainly because the staff action is an overestimation of the individual actual existing capability. Most DSP will not openly express their lack of understanding of an individual's full capability but instead they will make available a list of meaningful activities they have tried and failed with the individual. What is forgotten is that meaningfulness is not appropriateness, hence, no matter how meaningful an activity is, it become less significant when it is directed at a person who has no use of it.

Takeaway—29

It is a mistake to think that a task is complex in relation to the individual's capacity when the problem is actually that the task is a complete mismatch with or overestimation of the individual's capacity thus failing to take the whole individual into the planning process.

An individual can perform any task or activity that is uniquely tailored to his skills and preference

➢ Consider another example: If the task requires passing the beading wire through a bead, it must be such that the task is the individual's preference and the individual has some basic skill such as holding the beading wire in one hand and the bead in another, and direct support is only needed to be applied regularly or as much as needed to help the individual accomplish the task independently overtime. But when the individual is challenged with the first basic fine motor skills then the bead task is not the first way forward but rather providing support directed at enhancing the fine motor skill then the bead task will be more logical.

Takeaway—30

When a task is designed around the individual's current skill set it is less likely that the individual will be found to lack the capacity required to complete that task.

D

Summary of Chapter

1. The development of the individual must center on his ability, and on his preferences (not on what is expected of him except he is being paid for meeting the expectations such as in an employment or under some other arrangement). The things that the individual can naturally do with little help are an asset to start with in the direct support process. Exposure also helps with discovering some of those things. The frequent and relevant the exposure the more the set of preferences increases.

    Therefore, when exposure is based around the ability of the individual, subsequent preference formed will be less challenging to accomplish.

2. Expectations play essential role in expanding an individual's existing sets of preference by exposing him to more experiences so as to help him in forming more specific preferences.

    However, a skill must not be built around the expectations because of the broad open-ended nature of expectations and their tendencies to overwhelm the capability.

3. If an expectation is condensed into a preference but the resulting preference is not within the capacity of the individual, DSP must shift the focus of the experiences that the individual has been exposed as a result of the preference. DSP must ensure that the experience affords the individual some types of role other than mere exposure to partial participation.

4. Results are based on the actions that fuel them. If an action is appropriate planned with a realistic expectation in mind, the result appropriate to the action will be certain.

The complete ramifications of an individual's involvement must be considered especially when the individual's participation is the first of such in a community opportunity.

We tend to ignore or pretend as though failure doesn't exist sometimes out of the wishful thinking that thinking anything other than positive will impede positive from occurring.

5. DSP must properly record the preferences of the individual so as to maintain a resource manual that can be used as a reference as the more information there is about what the individual likes the richer the direct support process will be.

6. It is a mistake to think that a task is complex in relation to the individual's capacity when the problem is actually that the task is a complete mismatch with or overestimation of the individual's capacity thus failing to take the whole individual into the planning process.

7. When a task is designed around the individual's current skill set it is less likely that the individual will be found to lack the capacity required to complete that task.

Appendix

The Case of Wendy Johns

Objective:

- To apply the appropriate tools to the sample habilitation case of Wendy Johns

This appendix contains a real day habilitation case. The tools discussed in this book that are relevant to the case are applied so as to provide a practical understanding of how the tools can be used. The hypothetic location is the Ginger Bread Adult Day Habilitation Center. It is the case of Wendy Johns. The Ginger Bread Adult Day Habilitation Center is one of three program locations of the Ginger Bread Community Foundation for people who are intellectual and developmentally challenged. Wendy Johns was transferred to the Ginger Bread Adult Day Habilitation Center from another day program also in Ginger Bread Community known as the Sprinkleland Complaint Care.

As a procedure for the transfer all relevant documentations were sent to the Ginger Bread center. Prior to starting, the Ginger Bread program manager, Ms. Ali, phoned and spoke with all relevant parties about holding a team meeting to discuss the services that Wendy will be receiving at Ginger Bread and to find ways to make the transition less stressful for her considering that Wendy had spent considerable length of time at the previous program. After reviewing available documents for Wendy, Ms. Ali suggested that the DSP who has been working with Wendy at the previous program should be present at the meeting.

Ms. Ali drew a summary from the transferred documents for Wendy as follows:

Wendy is senior citizen who is nonverbal and does not understand sign language. Wendy understands few action words when spoken to her such as come, let's go, "bathroom", eat, have a seat, and put on your coat. Other than responding to those action words, she does not respond to any other communication involving explanation of actions or to questions in any manner as she is able to do gesture like nodding. However, if Wendy is in disagreement of an "action word" she would not perform it. For instance if a DSP said to Wendy, please have a seat, Wendy would not sit if she does not agree with sitting in the particular space.

Wendy had recently underwent refractive surgery to improve her eye sight and it is recommended by her doctor that she must be protected from conditions that would cause irritation to her eye such as windy and dusty environs. No adaptive glasses are prescribed for her. Wendy does not walk more than two blocks regardless of weather conditions. Wendy feeds herself and does most ADL on her own. She enjoys striking the piano keyboard as there is a family piano at home which she enjoys playing with. According to her sister, Wendy clears the table after meals at home, and occasionally she can get her own cereal in the morning. At her previous program, Wendy displayed no behaviors of concern and she is usually in agreement with almost every suggestion that DSP makes on her behalf as far engaging in activities and going on community trips are concern.

Ms. Ali also noted that that the previous program and Wendy's family have not identified anything that Wendy dislikes. She is very agreeable. Wendy does make some grinding sounds but she does it so often and randomly that it is difficult to tie it to anything in her surrounding or to be a reaction to a staff action. Wendy is physically stable and requires no physical support.

From the above fact, Ms. Ali needs to know what preference Wendy would adopt for herself if she could express it. Ms. Ali knows that making wild guesses is not an option. But since Wendy is nonverbal and at this time Wendy cannot express what she would like to be supported on, Ms. Ali and the team will need to determine what preference can be inferred from Wendy's action and support cycle?

The transferred documentations seem to identify what Wendy does at home and some description of her personality. However, most importantly, in order to provide the appropriate service to Wendy, Ms. Ali will need to figure out all of the things that Wendy likes as much as possible.

On the day of the meeting, Ms. Ali collected all of the tools she needed to collect the information she must have to devise a day habilitation plan for Wendy. The tools that Ms. Ali had prepared herself with included the following:

- The **SEAMAN** Implied Preference Form
  o **SEAMAN** is the acronym from *Safety, Empowerment, Ability, Manifested Need, Agreement,* and *Medical*

For nonverbal individuals; Indicate how preferences were adopted

Safety	Empowerment	Ability	Manifested Needs	Agreement/ consensus	Medical/Clinical
(Current concern for Physical and psychological wellbeing)	*(Past and current experiences from which enhancement and empowerment were gained)*	*(Existing capabilities that would make performance possible)*	*(unnegotiable daily necessities of the individual across relevant settings)*	*(specify issues for which there is consensus of the family, guardian, and/or advocate)*	*(most recent clinical and medical situation of the individual)*

2A	**Implied Preferences**
	It is implied that:
1.	
2.	
3.	

- **The Now Factor Skills** form
  - o The Now Factor is a skill formulated based on the existing capacity of the individual

Existing Capabilities	Expectations	Preferences/Goal	TNF Skill
(see Section 2)		*(See Section 2A for Implied Preference)*	*("The Now Factor" Skill)*

Those two forms are what Ms. Ali needs to fill out at the meeting in the presence of the team so as to ensure a consensual team effort. Now after filling out the forms at the meeting, Ms. Ali proceeded to complete the day habilitation plan for Wendy Johns using all of the information available to her:

Ginger Bread Adult Day Habilitation Center
123 Main Park, New York
Group Day Habilitation Plan

Name:	Wendy Johns	Medicaid #:	W123XXXXX
Date Updated:	4/30/2014 *(this is the date that the meeting was held from which this plan was created.)*	Date Implemented:	4/21/2014 *(this is the date that service was authorized for Wendy Johns at Ginger Bread; same as date of enrollment)*

1. Individual Profile: *(use bullet for each significant information)*

A. General information	B. Safeguards/Current level of support	C. Challenges/Needs
Wendy • conducts ADL on her own; and goes to the bathroom when she feels like it • goes to church regularly • cleans after herself after meal at home • enjoys community trips and going to the mall • enjoys watching TV at home • enjoys listening to music; and began loving YouTube since the surgery • always neatly dressed • always reacts to action words including come, let's go, *bathroom*, cat, have a seat, and put on your coat • May refuse to react to action words when in disagreement.	• Must always be within the presence of a DSP as she could be taken advantage of due to her inability to communicate overtly • Difficulty walking more than 2 city blocks at any given time. • Not travel trained; cannot travel independently • History of refractive surgery • Cannot exit building independently during fire and other emergency	• Nonverbal/may benefit from sign language • Wendy's social skill is difficult to access as she is very quiet/may benefit from social skills training • Wendy has not been exposed to gaining money management skills

Current Valued	*VO#1:*	Wendy would like to interact more with DSP.	*Skill #1:*	Wendy will learn to indicate to DSP when she wants help with something.

Outcome & Skills			
	VO#2:	Wendy would like to be able to signal when she is going to the restroom.	Skill #2:	Wendy will learn to sign bathroom to DSP when she wants to go to the bathroom.
	VO#3:	Wendy would like to live a healthy life.	Skill #3:	Wendy will learn to choose more fruit snacks over sugary foods.

Summarize changes occurring since last review:
(indicate challenges, progress, & any new discoveries)

Wendy was transferred to Ginger Bread center because of Ginger Bread center's proximity to Wendy's home. Before the transfer, no other challenge was observed other than those indicated under section C of this profile. No new discovery has been noted since the last review.

2. For nonverbal individual; indicate how preferences were adopted

Safety (Current concern for Physical and psychological wellbeing)	Empowerment (Past and current experiences from which enhancement and empowerment were gained)	Ability (Existing capabilities that would make performance possible)	Medical/Clinical (most recent clinical and medical situation of the individual)	Agreement/consensus (specify issues for which there is a consensus of the family, guardian, and/or advocate)	Needs Manifested (unnegotiable daily necessities of the individual across relevant settings)
1. Ensuring Wendy is not taken advantage of due to her inability to communicate overtly 2. Cannot walk more than 2 city blocks at any given time.	1. Clearing meal table at home 2. Feeding herself	1. Ability to follow action words 2. Ability to not follow action words when in disagreement 3. Fairly independent ADL skills 4. Able to strike piano keyboard 5. Feeds herself once she is served 6. Clears meal table at home 7. Gets along with DSP and group members	Refractive surgery – must be protected from windy and dusty environs to avoid irritation of the eye	Wendy's sister wants Wendy to improve on: 1. Serving herself with cold food like salad, cereal; 2. Clearing the table at least after herself 3. Learning to sign simple words relevant to her routine *Note: Wendy's sister is only family left who is involved with servicer providers, and has been directly involved with Wendy for 10 years.*	1. Communicate with DSP 2. Learning sign language

2A. Implied Preferences

1. Given that Wendy performs action words but unable to express her disagreement, she would benefit from learning sign language for basic everyday words relevant to her routine.
2. Considering that Wendy is able to feed herself once she is served, she would benefit from learning to make cold lunches such as sandwich on her own.
3. Since Wendy currently cleans after herself after a meal, however, she spills stuff from the table to the floor because of which she would benefit from improving on that skill to clean properly after meals.

3. Indicate rationale for change in skills to be attained:

Existing Capabilities (see Section 2)	Expectations (from family's desire/wish, guardian/advocate; self)	Preferences/Goal (See Section 2A for Implied Preference)	TNF Skill ("The Now Factor" Skill)
Ability to follow action words	To communicate with others	To communicate using sign language	To increase her understanding of more action words while also learning her sign language
Feeds herself once she is served	To make her own meal	To make cold sandwich, and cereal	To learn to make her own cold sandwich and cereal.
Clears meal table at home	To clear the table and not waste stuff on the floor	To be able to clean after self properly after meal	To learn to clean after herself properly after meal.
Fairly independent ADL skills			
Able to strike piano keyboard			
Gets along with DSP and group member			
Clears meal table at home			
Ability to not follow action words when in disagreement	To communicate with others		

Note after matching the number of Implied Preferences against the appropriate existing capability the rest of the capabilities can remain listed on this form for ongoing references.

Check if Revised ☒ Starting 06/01/2014   Check if Revised ☒ Starting 06/01/2014   To learn sign language for basic

4.A.	Services #1:	Communication	Goal #1:	everyday words relevant to her
	(based on Expressed or Implied preference)		*(based on Expressed or Implied preference)*	routine.

Skills to be attained: *Insert TNF Skill here*
(identify the skills in the order of relevance to the goal)

- To increase her understanding of more action words while also learning her sign language

Check all that apply
Skills intended to address/provide:
☒ **Skill Acquisition/Retention**
☐ **Staff Support**   ☒ **Exploration of New Experiences**

Staff Actions:
(must be based on Needs, Autonomy, Methodology, & Opportunity)

- DSP will introduce more new action words to Wendy by having regular conversations during daily interaction relevant to her routine.
- DSP will begin demonstrating new sign language of basic words to Wendy by signing some of the action words that Wendy is already familiar with.

| 4.B. | Check if Revised ☒ Starting 06/01/2014 Services #2: *(based on Expressed or Implied preference)* | Pursuing Valued Outcome | Check if Revised ☒ Starting 06/01/2014 Goal #2: *(based on Expressed or Implied preference)* | To learn to make cold lunches such as sandwich on her own. |

Skills to be attained: *Insert TNF Skill here*
(identify the skills in the order of relevance to the goal)

- To learn to make her own cold sandwich and cereal.

Check all that apply
Skills intended to address/provide:
☒ Skill Acquisition/Retention
☐ Staff Support   ☒ Exploration of New Experiences

Staff Actions:
(must be based on Needs, Autonomy, Methodology, & Opportunity)

- DSP will introduce sandwich ingredients to Wendy starting with her favorite kind of sandwich during lunch time.
- DSP will demonstrate making cereal to Wendy using Wendy choice of cereal during the morning at program.

| 4.C. | Check if Revised ☒ Starting 06/01/2014 Services #3: *(based on Expressed or Implied preference)* | Housekeeping | Check if Revised ☒ Starting 06/01/2014 Goal #3: *(based on Expressed or Implied preference)* | To improve on her skill to clean properly after meals. |

Skills to be attained: *Insert TNF Skill here*
(identify the skills in the order of relevance to the goal)

- To learn to clean after self properly after meal.

Check all that apply
Skills intended to address/provide:
☒ Skill Acquisition/Retention
☐ Staff Support   ☐ Exploration of New Experiences

Staff Actions:
(must be based on Needs, Autonomy, Methodology, & Opportunity)

- DSP will have regular conversation with Wendy and use more familiar action words such as clean, remove, wipe, empty in garbage.

Name of Staff Completing Plan _____   **Title:** _____

      Date Completed   4/30/2014   **Signature:** _____

Confirmation of internal distribution & filling
☐ Service Coordinator: _____   *Signature*

Glossary

Direct Support Terms

Ability The existing capability and willingness relevant to performing a given task.

Acknowledgement (1) The show of understanding and appreciation to the individual's or DSP's effort at staying on course of a plan or for the achievement of a milestone; (2) also one of the elements of maintaining consistency in staff action.

Action (1) Any act in the course of direct support process or that which requires direct support; (2) one of the parts of a routine which refers to the activity of the routine.

Active attention A personalized consideration that is rendered in listening and responding to an individual in a way that expresses unconditional interest in the individual.

Animated Response An active response that is marked by progress and spirited expression exemplifying the individual's awareness of both the event or task at hand and the surrounding in which it is taking place.

Appropriate Refers to relevance in terms of both age and capability.

145

Arrival time The time that the individual receiving services reaches the service location.

Artificial routine A routine that is formed from preferences or learnt behavior including all of those undertakings that occur as a result of the individual's past exposures and current inclination.

Autonomy The individual's sense of self, empowerment, independence, and safety.

Branching Out An approach of gradually expanding on the individual's routine by exposure to new experiences relevant the existing capability

Brokerage An attempt at initiating or brokering personal engagement with the individual through stimulation, negotiation, facilitation and taking practical actions relevant to the objective of the engagement.

Capability The individual's ability based upon which a preference materializes.

Challenge (1) Refers to the practical roadblock that obstructs the application of a staff action or that which hinders engagement with the individual; (2) a barrier to the formulation of a more individualized staff action.

Circumstance The event or action similar to those in which the target skill will more likely occur.

Community inclusion   An exposure to the unrestricted public spaces that are opened to every community member.

Community integration   The assimilation into the community through inclusion and participation that is meant to enhance the sense of belonging

Community participation   The process of taking part in community activities through contribution including other maximum use of the community

Consequence   The ramification of the result of an action in the direct support process including staff action and those of the individual.

Consistency   The uniform regularity that is required to ensuring congruity and continuity in the effort formulated to support delivery of a staff action.

Constellation of tasks   An interconnection of actions that are related to the individual's specific preference providing a sequential depiction of order of the tasks necessary to achieve the goal.

Contact   The groundwork of engagement and the initial line of interaction with an individual as a way of knowing how the individual feels at any given point of the engagement

Customize   To tailor supports and interaction to the unique needs of the individual.

Derived Events (1) Events that produce community integration as an outcome; (2) a form of exposure that is only concentrated toward community integration involving both community inclusion and participation.

Dexterity The individual's mastery of a task as a result of consistent practice and a handy staff action.

Direct Discovery Refers to any observation or findings encountered through direct interactions with individuals receiving service

Direct support (1) An art of engagement concentrated toward safeguarding and empowering a person receiving applied support services; (2) prearranged help directed at enhancing an individualized goal.

Direct support process A practice of continuously evolving engagement with an individual embedded with simulation based on both the individual's level of ongoing development and the manifested needs for assistance.

Discovery Findings through observation and interaction with an individual that furthers or hinders the staff action and the direct support process as a whole

Dismissal time The time that the individual receiving services departs the service location.

Effectiveness	(1) The usefulness of the staff action in advancing the individual toward the target goal; (2) the efficiency at preventing the individual from regressing away from the target goal
Empowerment	One of the goals of direct support emphasizing enhancement through exposures and bringing the individual toward independence in both personal livelihood and community integration.
Encouragement	Reinforcement or reassurances that draws the individual back to a given task or motivates him into increased involvement.
Engagement	Connecting and interacting with the individual with the goal of providing or enhancing direct support process.
Enhancement	(1) Boosting or improving an action or response to an action in the direct support process; (2) anything or action that appropriately enriches the individual's experience.
Existing capacity	(1) The prerequisite skills based upon which new preferences and skill must be formulated; (2) current ability.
Expectation	(1) The hopes and aspirations that are desired for or by the individual; (2) the things that are hoped for the individual to accomplish; (3) the probability of all of those things and possibilities for which there is a vision for fulfillment.

Experience The individual's involvement with past events or exposure to new ones; or the individual's familiarity with the conduct of a task or activity.

Exposure Introduction to a new experience or to facilitate an individual's repeated experience with an event or task.

Facilitation The effort that is enabling and necessary for utilizing the circumstances surrounding a staff action more effectively.

Family Expectation Hopes and aspiration expressed by the family for the individual to accomplish.

Frequency of routine The span of the routine that provides understanding into the regularity at which the routine occurs.

Function One of the parts of a routine which refers to the manner in which the activity is carried out as well as the purpose or meaning derived from carrying out the activity.

Genuine care The unconditional support demonstrated during engagement with the individual.

Goal The object towards which staff actions are directed.

Genuine Routine   Natural and ritualistic undertaking by an individual on commitment bases as a demonstration of behavioral or habitual ramifications of a natural state.

Hard Contact   Contact involving a physical act such as a touch that results in getting the individual's attention; also includes those contacts that produce concrete response from the individual such as sound and sight.

Identify & profile opportunities   A principle of engagement that involves recognizing the routine and breaking it down in segments that will enable fuller understanding of the routine in the effort to smoothen the engagement process.

Impression   Our thoughts and feelings about the individual receiving services.

Level of support   The amount of oversight and degree of assistance required by the individual relevant to the individual's unique conditions

Make Connection   A principle of engagement that emphasizes among other things persisting on caring and connecting with the individual's existing connections.

Manifested Needs   Nonnegotiable daily necessities of the individual across relevant settings. *Also the same as needs manifested.*

Manufactured image   (1) The faulty representations formed in our minds about the individual receiving services; (2) a notion about the individual that is far from the reality of the individual

Meaningful   (1) An experience, interaction, or activity that is empowering; (2) any action or activity that has features that would contribute to the enhancement of the individual or lead to a positive experience.

Methodology   Definite and realistic steps relevant to attaining or maintaining a specified skill.

Milestone   An accomplishment toward the individualized goal.

Missed Opportunity   (1) A failure to explore occurrence of the routine; (2) the result of the lack of consistency in exploring and engaging the individuals in their routines.

Muted Response   A suppressed reaction displayed as a result of some unfolding situations obstructing the individual's active involvement.

Needs   Nonnegotiable necessities of the individual across relevant settings

Negotiation   (1) Discussion about plans of preferred daily actions or of exposure to resources and experiences related to the goal; (2) a communication between the DSP and individual to find a common ground around how to proceed with the engagement.

Opportunity	A series of daily living interactions, that when consistently explored, leads either to the attainment of emerging skills or maintenance of current ones.
Overemphasizing	The tendency to exaggerate situation, response, or reaction from the individual.
Overlooking	The tendency to willfully ignore or to utterly disregard the situation, response, or reaction from the individual.
Partial participation	A role on the part of the individual in which the individual takes no action other than being present with the exception of where the sole performance of the task is the same as the presence of the individual.
Patience	(1) The demonstration of persistence and endurance in the application of a staff action as well as in interaction with the individual; (2) One of the key pillar of maintaining consistency in the direct support process.
Persist on Caring	A sub-element of making connection with the individual's existing connection which expresses through action of unconditional interest in engaging and provided targeted help to the individual.
Personal expectation	(1) Hopes and aspiration that the individual personally expresses or acts upon as a way of making known what he hopes to have; (2) some other requirement of the individual.

Preference (1) An individual's choice expressed based on past experiences or on encounters with new and ongoing exposures; (2) choices inferred from either the individual's action, the unique circumstances surrounding the individual's current situation or from the individual's past history of similar preferences.

Prompt A signal for the initiation or continuation of a task dispensed with either a sign, guidance, stimulation, or encouragement given to the individual in a way that is uniquely understood and appreciated by the individual

Protection Safeguarding the individual physical and emotional wellbeing

Requisite skills The initial skill or set of skills needed to initiate a task; the existing capability upon which a preference or goal is set.

Result The eventuality that occurs as the particular ramification of a staff action.

Reverse Constellation The process of replacing the relationship between acts or events that lead to a harmful or disruptive behavior with events that will serve a constructive role to the person's overall wellbeing

Routine	(1) A specific ongoing interactions that is usually built up from an individual's preference; (2) some ongoing behavioral or habitual happening occurring as part of a natural state of the individual
Safeguards	The protective steps or measures put in place to ensure or stabilize the individual wellbeing.
Safety	The welfare of the individual that especially requires protection and guidance away from acts or condition that threatens or that has the propensity to threaten the individual's wellbeing and security.
Scenario	Example of situation relevant to the issue at hand; a setup or creation of such situation.
Scenario of Opportunity	Refers to the time, environment, and special occurrence of a routine that makes the routine more predictable.
Service Provider's expectation	An incorporation of the individual's personal expectations and that of the family, as well as those expectations that reflect the trends in the field to include any new definitions of terms and requirement for service provision to comply with.
Skills	The capability needed to act on a preference or an exposure.

Soft Contact   (1) A contact that involves emotional or mental stimulation that results in getting the individual's attention; (2) contacts mostly based on direct or indirect communication about things of interest to the individual

Spontaneity   Unstructured and unplanned involvement of the individual in an activity with the flexibility to get into or out of the event at any point of the interaction

Staff action   A definite attempt at providing prearranged services directed at protecting or empowering or both by taking timely and measureable steps that enhances the skill necessary to achieving the individualized goal.

Staged Participation   The arrangement for performance whereby the event or task is divided amongst the people working to complete it, and divided in a way that the absence of any one part will not make a complete whole of the task.

Stimulation   Inspiring or motivating the individual into taking part in an activity or some other arrangement

Technical Discovery   (1) The kinds of developments that are clinical or those findings that are not immediate results of direct staff actions; (2) developments that shift the overall policies and approaches to service types and delivery at agency, local, state, and federal levels.

Transit routine   A brief routine that occurs between events or tasks and is usually the individual way of transitioning.

Tunnel routine   Lengthier interaction on the part of the individual that is more prolonged.

Valued Outcome   The result towards which the staff actions are directed.

Virtual Disconnect   The non-relationship between a current goal and a newly expressed or implied goal.